A Teacher's Guide to

TORAH
The Growing Gift

A Teacher's Guide to

TORAH
The Growing Gift

Steven E. Steinbock

UAHC Press
New York, New York

Contents

Torah: The Growing Gift and Its Teacher's Guide

ABOUT THE TEXTBOOK

Welcome to *A Teacher's Guide to Torah: The Growing Gift*. The text introduces students in grades 3 to 5 to the study of the Torah, the Five Books of Moses. Each chapter presents selected Torah texts, along with creative learning activities that are designed to teach young readers how to interpret the Torah for themselves. All text selections have been newly translated with a sensitivity to accuracy and gender-neutral language, making them ideal for young readers.

The textbook's goal is to help the students gain Jewish insights through Torah study. In the course of the school year, as the students develop Torah study skills, they will gain an increasing knowledge of the key themes, values, and wisdom found in the Torah. The students will learn how to apply this growing body of knowledge to their own life and family situation. Through exploring the stories and *mitzvot* contained in the Torah, the students will begin to develop a lifelong appreciation for and commitment to Talmud Torah.

Three key objectives are presented sequentially in the textbook in order to facilitate the students' growing understanding. The text helps facilitate the students' ability to (1) identify and interpret symbols used in the Torah; (2) identify moral acts of biblical characters and distinguish between moral and immoral acts in contemporary life; and (3) identify sacred experiences recounted in the Torah and perceive sacred experiences in the course of the students' daily life. Each of these objectives is explored from different perspectives throughout the textbook with increasing complexity as the students work through the chapters.

How the Textbook Is Organized

The text consists of 23 chapters. In addition, the book features an introduction and a conclusion. Each chapter—which contains background information, one or more Torah texts, and creative learning activities—is designed as a learning unit and provides sufficient material for one or more lessons. The chart on pages 112 to 117 provides an overview of the biblical texts and activities contained in each chapter. Space is provided for you to schedule each lesson for the school year.

ABOUT THE TEACHER'S GUIDE

A Teacher's Guide to Torah: The Growing Gift is a detailed plan to help you effectively present each chapter of the textbook. The guide suggests teaching strategies, includes the correct answers to the questions in the textbook, and presents alternate methods of class management for the use of the activities found in the text.

How the Teacher's Guide Is Organized

Each chapter of the teacher's guide, which corresponds to a chapter in the textbook, is divided into the sections described below. The following guidelines will help you develop one or more lessons per chapter. Each chapter of the teacher's guide contains the following seven components:

Chapter Summary A short synopsis of the chapter, providing overview and highlights of the contents.

Objectives A selection of suggested behavioral learning objectives to use as a basis for developing your lesson. These objectives should serve as a guide for selecting learning activities and discussion topics and also as an evaluative gauge of students' accomplishments.

Major Themes A list of the key topics or ideas presented in the chapter.

Key Terms A list of the terms, words, and/or concepts used or introduced in the chapter.

Background for the Teacher A variety of points that are (1) commonly misunderstood and/or (2) crucial for student mastery of the material. Be sure to read these points carefully and incorporate them into your lesson. It is highly recommended that teachers refer to *The Torah: A Modern Commentary* edited by W. Gunther Plaut (New York: UAHC Press, 1981) for additional background and commentary.

Methodology A number of sequential learning activities intended for use with the chapter. Each lesson includes these components: (1) Introduction; (2) Learning Activities—the core activities for teaching a lesson; and (3) Closure—closing the lesson. In addition, **Enrichment Activities** are included to help you expand the lesson.

USING *TORAH: THE GROWING GIFT*: OVERALL STRATEGIES

Torah: The Growing Gift is a classroom-ready, user-friendly tool for teaching and learning Torah. The text, discussions, and activities were designed to guide you and your students through the contents and themes of the Five Books of Moses. Since each lesson flows directly from the readings and activities in the text, you need only guide the students through the readings and activities in order to fulfill the lesson objectives. The following lesson-planning strategies explain the classroom preparations you will need to make and how you can "shape" the lessons.

As the teacher, you have several options for how you will organize each lesson. Choose the options that most closely match your philosophy and style or experiment with one or more of them. Options include:

- Lead the class in an oral reading of each chapter, with the students taking turns reading the Torah texts, paragraph by paragraph. You may stop briefly to allow the students to complete questions and activities. This option enables the teacher to actively prompt and guide the students and to answer students' questions as they arise.

- Assign chapters as homework to be read and completed before the class meets. The classroom lesson can then focus on discussions and completing additional enrichment activities.

- Devote time at the beginning of each class to silent individual reading. Follow with discussions and additional learning activities.

- Have the students read the Torah texts and complete the activities in pairs or small groups.

The following outline lists the essential steps to take in teaching each lesson, followed by details about each step.

A. Introduction The lessons that your students will remember best will be those that begin creatively. Choose an opening that will grab your students' attention, highlight the main themes of the lesson, introduce the major concepts and vocabulary included in the lesson, and/or relate the theme(s) of the chapter to the students' lives.

B. Learning Activities

1. The students read from *Torah: The Growing Gift* based on one or more of the reading model options presented above.

2. Pose questions that elicit students' curiosity. Open the floor to questions about the content of the chapter.

3. Guide students through the activities in the text.

4. Focus on the pictures. Use the illustrations in the text to deepen the students' understanding of various concepts. Tell the students to pay attention to the pictures. Ask questions that will encourage the students to make connections between their newly acquired knowledge and the pictures. For example, ask the students what the illustration on the title page depicts. (the Ark of the Covenant) Use the pictures to pique students' curiosity and broaden their knowledge.

C. Closure Don't leave the lesson open-ended. Conclude the lesson with a review discussion. Reemphasize (or better yet, have the students reemphasize) the key points and terms of the chapter. Use this time to expand on the Torah texts through a follow-up enrichment assignment. Promote creative interpretation of the texts by using dramatic projects (e.g., role-playing, dramatic readings, audio drama, video performance, etc.), as well as plastic arts (e.g., painting, murals, models, reconstructions, etc.).

God's Gift of Learning

Introduction Summary

The opening chapter of *Torah: The Growing Gift* introduces Torah as a concept as well as a document. *Torah* means "Teaching" or "Direction." But Torah is also a scroll, a book, a set of five books, a set of teachings, a collection of stories, a gift from God to the Jewish people, and a Tree of Life.

Objectives

• Explain how the Torah is a scroll, a book, five books, Jewish teachings, a collection of stories, and a gift.

• Explain how the Torah is a Tree of Life.

• Identify the names of the Five Books of Moses and tell what they mean.

• Define *mitzvah* as a Jewish responsibility and give examples of *mitzvot* in modern life and Jewish tradition.

Major Themes

• *Torah* means "Teaching" and usually refers to the Five Books of Moses.

• The Torah can be understood as the biography of the Jewish people. But its stories are not just about people who died a long time ago. Every story in the Torah is about each one of us—you and me—and is relevant to our lives.

• The Torah is a symbol of the relationship between God and the Jewish people, a relationship based on commitment and love.

Key Terms

Torah
תּוֹרָה

"Teaching" or "Instruction." All Jewish ethical and spiritual teachings in general. Specifically, the Five Books of Moses, the *Chumash*.

Sefer Torah
סֵפֶר תּוֹרָה

A handwritten scroll containing the Five Books of Moses.

Sofer
סוֹפֵר

A Hebrew scribe. One who writes and/or checks *Sifrei Torah*, Torah scrolls, as well as *mezuzah* and *tefilin* parchments.

Yad
יָד

"Hand" or "arm." A pointer stick, usually shaped like a small human hand with a pointed index finger, used to assist in reading the Torah.

Mitzvah
מִצְוָה

A Jewish responsibility or "commandment." Any of the 613 instructions found in the Torah.

Genesis
בְּרֵאשִׁית

Greek for "Birth" or "Origin." The first of the Five Books of Moses. Its Hebrew name is Bereshit, which means "In the Beginning" or "When [God] Began."

Exodus
שְׁמוֹת

Greek for "Departure." The second of the Five Books of Moses. Its Hebrew name is Shemot, which means "Names," from its opening verse "These are the names...."

Leviticus
וַיִּקְרָא

Greek for "Priestly," from the Hebrew *Levi*, the priestly tribe. The third of the Five Books of Moses. Its Hebrew name is Vayikra, which means "And [God] Called."

Numbers
בְּמִדְבַּר

An English word that refers to the statistical data found in the fourth of the Five Books of Moses. Its Hebrew name is Bemidbar, which means "In the Desert."

Deuteronomy
דְּבָרִים

Greek for "Second Law." The fifth and last of the Five Books of Moses. Its Hebrew name is Devarim, which means "Words" or "Things," from the verse "These are the words that Moses said to Israel...."

Background for the Teacher

1. The word *Torah* is one of the central concepts of Judaism, yet it is frequently mistranslated and misunderstood. The word *Torah* means "Teaching" or "Instruction." This is the name given to the Five Books of Moses, known in Hebrew as the *Chumash* and in Greek as *Pentateuch*. But the term *Torah* may also refer to the wider realm of Jewish learning and religious writings.

   Torah is sometimes incorrectly translated as "The Law." While the Torah contains many rules, regulations, and responsibilities, the word *Torah* has nothing to do with law. The primary purpose of the Torah is to educate, not to legislate.

The term *Torah* is sometimes applied to the entire Jewish Bible. But the Torah is just part of the Jewish Bible. The Hebrew Bible, called *Tanach* in Hebrew and the Old Testament by Christians, consists of twenty-four books (according to some Jewish sources; others count thirty-nine books), of which the Torah comprises the first five.

2. The word *mitzvah* means "commandment" and may be understood as a Jewish responsibility. It comes from the root צ-ו-ה, meaning "to command." While many *mitzvot* involve kind acts, it is misleading and inaccurate to translate the word *mitzvah* as a "good deed."

3. Who wrote the Torah? Jews differ in their explanations as to who wrote the Torah and how it was written. Some Jews believe that each word of the Torah was dictated by God to Moses at Sinai, ca. 1200 B.C.E. Others believe that the Torah is derived from several older sources, written by a variety of scholars and priests—known as J, E, and P, ca. 800-500 B.C.E.—and compiled into its present form by an editor known as D. The beliefs of most Reform Jews rest somewhere between these opinions. We all agree that regardless of how the text actually came to be, it is holy because it reflects human striving to understand God. According to Rabbi W. Gunther Plaut, "The Torah is ancient Israel's distinctive record of its search for God. It attempts to record the meeting of the human and the Divine, the great moments of encounter. Therefore, the text is often touched by the ineffable Presence." (*The Torah: A Modern Commentary*, page xix) For more about this subject, see Ellen Singer, *Our Sacred Texts* (New York: UAHC Press, 1993, pages 11 to 14) and Eugene Borowitz, *Understanding Judaism* (New York: UAHC Press, 1981, pages 123 to 131).

Methodology

Introduction

1. Before you begin the Introduction, make a Torah display. Include a Torah scroll; a copy of *The Torah: A Modern Commentary;* a copy of *Torah: The Five Books of Moses* (JPS); a *Tikkun* (a reader's copy of the Torah); a set of *Mikraot Gedolot* (Torah with rabbinic commentary); a Sephardic Torah scroll in a wooden case, miniature plastic models of which can be bought in Israel. Give the students the opportunity to examine and handle each of the items on display and ask questions about them.

Learning Activities

2. Have the students learn the names and meanings of the items that decorate a *Sefer Torah*. In addition to the *yad*, these include the *keter, rimonim, atzei chayim* (rolling sticks), *choshen* (breastplate), *chagorah* (belt), and *ketonet* (mantle). Undress and open the Torah. Examine the parchment (*klaf*) and the writing with the students. Then redress the Torah.

3. Have the students read "God's Gift of Learning" on page 1 and "A Book," "A Scroll," and "Five Books" on page 2 in the textbook.

4. Have the students examine a copy of *The Holy Scriptures* (Philadelphia: JPS, 1962). Compare its contents to those of a Revised Standard Version of the Holy Bible. Locate the five books of the Torah in each version. Repeat this activity with Plaut's *The Torah: A Modern Commentary*, identifying the Torah material and distinguishing it from the commentaries, footnotes, and *haftarah* sections.

5. Have the students learn the Hebrew names for the Five Books of Moses. Examine the first verse of each of the books to identify the source of the Hebrew names. Compare the meanings of the Hebrew names with those of the Greek names for the books.

6. Have the students read "Jewish Teaching" on page 3 of the textbook. Pause for questions. Ask the students to name some *mitzvot*. List the examples that they give on the chalkboard. Emphasize the different types of behavior (ethical, ritual, family, business, etc.) that involve *mitzvot*.

7. Have the students read "A Book of Stories" on page 3 of the textbook. Ask the students which Torah stories they have learned in previous years (e.g., Noah's Ark, Joseph and the Coat of Many Colors, the Exodus, etc.).

   Note: The students may list stories that are not in the Torah (e.g., Jonah or Esther) as well as *midrashim*—(e.g. Abraham's Breaking of the Idols). Respond to these answers positively, pointing out that while these stories are *not* found in the Torah, they *are* part of the larger Jewish tradition.

8. Have the students read "A Very Special Gift" on page 3 of the textbook. After they have read that section, locate the *Shema* in a prayer book (in *Gates of Prayer,* edited by Chaim Stern, New York: CCAR, 1975, refer to page 130 for Shabbat evening and page 303 for Shabbat morning). Carefully read the prayer that immediately precedes the *Shema* (*Ahavat Olam* for evening and *Ahavah Rabbah* for morning) and the prayer that follows the *Shema,* the *Ve'ahavta*. Discuss how these prayers describe the words of the Torah as an expression of love between God and the Jewish people. Discuss ways in which education, rules, and responsibilities can be vehicles of love.

9. Have the students read and complete "A Tree of Life" on page 4 of the textbook. Then have the students share their answers and discuss some of the ways in which the Torah is a Tree of Life.

10. Have the students read the "Summary" on page 4 of the textbook. You may choose to invite questions in order to stimulate discussion.

Closure

11. Distribute construction paper and crayons, pencils, and/or pens. Have each student design a poster that promotes the value of Torah in Jewish life. Each poster should address several of the aspects of the Torah presented in the textbook and should include a slogan derived from the Tree of Life activity (see item 9, above).

Enrichment Activities

1. Invite a guest speaker who teaches about the role of a *sofer*, a scribe, and the task of writing Torah scrolls.

2. Read to the class from Nehemiah 8:1-8 in order to help the students understand the importance of the public reading of the Torah to the Jewish community after the Babylonian Exile, ca. 539 B.C.E. Compare this to the role of the public reading of the Torah today.

3. Examine one or more of the five Torah reading services in *Gates of Prayer*, pages 417 to 447. Identify and discuss the significance of taking out the Torah, the blessings said before and after the Torah is read, the Torah and *haftarah* readings, and the returning of the Torah to the ark.

4. Have the students participate in a Shabbat morning service (a Monday or Thursday morning service, or a reconstruction of such a service) that includes the public reading of the weekly Torah portion, the *parashah*.

5. Emphasize to the students that the study of Torah is a *mitzvah*. The Jewish people recite blessings, *berachot*, before engaging in many activities. The act of studying merits its own blessing: "Blessed are You, *Adonai* our God, Ruler of the universe, who makes us holy with *mitzvot* and commands us to engage in the study of Torah." This blessing is found on page 284 of *Gates of Prayer*.

Make a practice of reciting this blessing before you begin each class session. The students can compose a song using the words of this blessing or make a poster of this blessing for the classroom. The students can brainstorm to create a warm-up exercise that will help them direct their minds and hearts toward the study of Torah.

The Story of Creation

Chapter Summary

This chapter presents God's view of Creation with a reading from Genesis 1 about the seven days of Creation. The textbook stresses that God's Creation is orderly and good. The activities focus on the order of Creation, the idea that God created humankind "in the image of God," and Shabbat.

Objectives

- Identify a primary text of the Torah—referred to in this book as the Torah text—and distinguish between a primary text and commentary material in *Torah: The Growing Gift.*
- Relate acts of personal creativity to God's ongoing process of Creation.
- Analyze patterns in the story of Creation.
- Associate God's resting from the work of Creation on Shabbat with resting in one's own life.

Major Themes

- God brought order to the world during the seven days of Creation. The universe is not an accident. It evolved from chaos as a result of the planning and intention of the Creator.

- "And God saw that it was good." The world is a good place. Just as God appreciated everything in Creation, humans should respect and appreciate nature.

- Humankind was created in God's image.

- Shabbat is the seventh day, a day of rest.

Key Terms

Creation בְּרֵאשִׁית	The process of making something new. The Creation of the universe by God is described in Genesis.
Adam אָדָם	Hebrew for "human." Depending on the context, it refers to the Adam who lived in Eden or to all humanity.
Shabbat שַׁבָּת	The seventh day, a day of rest. Celebrated by Jews from Friday evening to Saturday night as a commemoration of God's Creation of the world.
Image צֶלֶם	A word that usually refers to a reproduction of the form of a person or thing, such as a picture or a statue. In *Torah: The Growing Gift* it refers mostly to mental pictures of things that cannot be reproduced, such as love, responsibility, and God.

Background for the Teacher

1. The students' first encounter with a Torah text occurs in this chapter. The Torah texts in *Torah: The Growing Gift* are translations that have been edited in such a way as to be both meaningful to the young reader and accurate with regard to the wording and meaning of the Hebrew text. Whenever possible and appropriate (i.e., when the text does not specifically refer to males or females), inclusive pronouns have been substituted for the traditional male pronouns. Redundancies have been omitted from the texts.

2. Throughout *Torah: The Growing Gift* the students are asked to give personal responses to items such as those in the "In the Image of God" activity on page 9. Encourage the students to give sincere responses to these exercises. Emphasize that there are no wrong answers.

3. The Hebrew word *Adam* is both a proper name and a noun that refers to all humanity. The Torah text in this chapter uses *Adam* in the second sense. In Chapter 1 *Adam* is used in both senses. *Adamah,* also from the word *Adam,* means "ground" or "earth." *Adam,* humanity, was created from the earth and is part of the natural world.

4. Anthropomorphism. God is not a person or a thing. No one can draw a picture or make a statue of God. God cannot be adequately described in words. But sometimes, in order to share information about God in a way that others can understand, we use human images to describe God. The process of using human characteristics, language, and images to describe something nonhuman is called anthropomorphism. The Bible often uses anthropomorphisms such as "God

said," "God made," "God saw," and "God rested" to help the reader understand God's actions. Sometimes the Bible ascribes human body parts to God so that the reader has a better frame of reference from which to understand God's actions. Although we know that God has no body and does not have a mouth, hands, or eyes, anthropomorphisms help give us an immediate (albeit simplistic) understanding of God, (see Enrichment Activity 3, below).

Methodology

Introduction

1. Discuss various creative activities that the students have participated in at school or at home. Generate a list of such activities. Explore the stages of creative activity (i.e., the steps that must be taken in order to create something: planning, constructing, fixing/repairing, enjoying the finished product, etc.).

Learning Activities

2. Point out to the students the lion icons on page 6 of the textbook. Explain that these lions tell the reader that the text that follows is a translation from the Torah. Explain to the students that in the Bible, lions are symbols for Judah, Saul, Jonathan, and even God. Representing bravery, majesty, and nobility, lions were early inhabitants of Palestine. Ask the students to describe the characteristics of lions and how these characteristics represent the Jewish people.

3. Have the students read the Torah text from Genesis 1 on pages 6 and 7 of the textbook. Elicit questions from the students and ask questions that pertain to the Torah text (e.g., "Which was created first: the trees or the land animals?" and "What did God tell people that they were responsible for?").

4. Review the directions for the activity on page 8 and have the students fill in the chart. After they have done so, have them share their answers with the class. You may choose to complete a similar chart on the chalkboard.

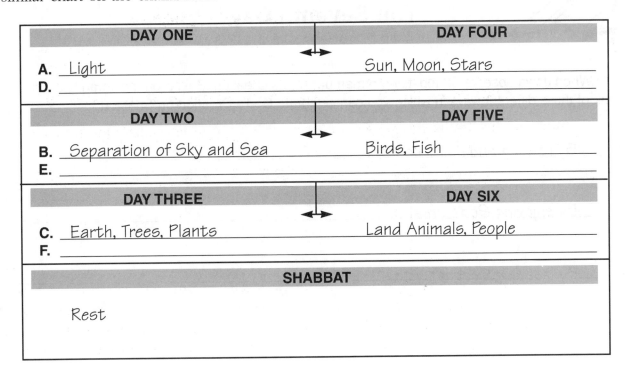

DAY ONE / DAY FOUR
A. Light / Sun, Moon, Stars
D.

DAY TWO / DAY FIVE
B. Separation of Sky and Sea / Birds, Fish
E.

DAY THREE / DAY SIX
C. Earth, Trees, Plants / Land Animals, People
F.

SHABBAT
Rest

Point out to the students that there is a pattern in the order of Creation. During the first three days of Creation, domains were established that corresponded to the objects or entities created on the following three days so that:

Day 1 (Light) corresponds to Day 4 (Sun, Moon, Stars)

Day 2 (Separation of Sky and Sea) corresponds to Day 5 (Sky Animals and Sea Animals)

Day 3 (Dry Land and Vegetation) corresponds to Day 6 (Land Animals and People)

5. Have the students read the section "In the Image of God" on page 9. Ask each student to share his or her responses with the class.

I am made in the image of God when I take care of the earth and all its creatures.	I see the image of God in other people when I watch them create drawings in art class.

6. Have the students complete "The Seventh Day" on page 9 and share their answers. As a class, have the students generate a list of Shabbat activities (candlelighting, synagogue attendance, family dinners, etc.). Discuss the lessons we can learn by observing these various *mitzvot* of Shabbat.

The Seventh Day

When Jews observe Shabbat, we remember God's Creation. Based on the Torah text, can you think of three different ways in which you can celebrate God's Creation on Shabbat?

1. By resting and doing no work

2. By enjoying God's creations

3. By blessing Shabbat

Closure

7. As a creative closing activity, have the students reenact the first week of the universe through art and/or drama.

Choose one or more of the following activities:

- Give each student a large piece of poster paper or butcher paper and tell the student to design a mural showing the days of Creation and the first Shabbat.

- Give each student a piece of construction paper and tell the student to depict one of the days of Creation in art. Display the completed art pieces on a wall or connect them with other works to form a scroll.

- Have the students work together on one or more class murals depicting the days of Creation and the first Shabbat.

- Students may wish to develop and present a Creation performance using a script they have written and dramatic/dance movements they have choreographed to depict the first week of the universe.

Enrichment Activities

1. Have the students participate in a short-term construction activity in class (such as making a model of their synagogue or of the ancient Temple) or assemble a piece of play equipment for children in the younger grades. Ask the students to discuss the phases of the creative process and how they felt as they created their projects.

2. Compare several translations of the opening verses of Genesis. See the King James Version, the Revised Standard Version, the Good News Bible, the JPS translation of the Bible, etc.

3. The Image of God. The notion that people are created in the image of God who is invisible may require a conceptual leap on the part of many students. God images used in the prayer book may help to clarify this concept.

God Images	**Human Images**
God is a Healer of the sick (from the *Amidah*).	A doctor who helps the sick.
God listens to prayer (from the *Amidah*).	A friend who listens to his or her friend.
God gives us Torah (from the Torah service).	A teacher who teaches ideas.
God makes us lie down in peace (from *Hashkivenu*).	A parent who tucks in his or her children at night.
God leads us to do holy acts through doing *mitzvot*.	We are holy when we do *mitzvot*.

4. Human Relationships and the Image of God. Use the following questions to stimulate discussion: "If everyone is created in God's image, are your parents made in the image of God? Are your brothers or sisters made in the image of God? Are your teachers made in the image of God? Are your friends made in the image of God? Are people whom you don't like very much also made in God's image? Ask the students: "Should you say something bad about someone who is made in the image of God? Should you hurt someone who is made in the image of God?"

Adam and Eve

Chapter Summary

This chapter tells the story of Adam and Eve and their expulsion from Eden, as well as the story of Cain and Abel. The activities focus on the use of symbols in the Torah and on distinguishing between right and wrong.

Objectives

- Define the word *symbol* as a word, picture, or image that helps us to understand abstract ideas or feelings.

- Extract and interpret Torah passages that make statements about the nature of humanity.

- Identify the Tree of Knowledge of Good and Bad as a symbol of moral awareness.

- Identify the Torah as a tool that helps us become more morally aware and understanding.

Major Themes

- The Torah often uses symbols to teach important values.

- The knowledge of right and wrong must be learned. Goodness does not come to us naturally but must be acquired. Torah and *mitzvot* are tools that help us learn what goodness is.

Key Terms

Symbol סֵמֶל, אוֹת	A word, picture, or image that stands for something else. Symbols help us to understand and communicate complicated or abstract ideas.
Tree of Life עֵץ חַיִּים	A tree planted by God in the Garden of Eden. (Genesis 2:9) Also a name used for the Torah. Possibly a symbol for eternal life. Possibly a symbol for the Torah.
Tree of Knowledge of Good and Bad עֵץ הַדַּעַת טוֹב וָרָע	A tree planted by God in Eden. (Genesis 2:9) Possibly a symbol for the awareness between right and wrong.
Morality/Ethics	Of or relating to principles of right and wrong in behavior.

Background for the Teacher

1. Morality. At this point, the students probably do not have a thorough understanding of the concept of morality. As they work through *Torah: The Growing Gift*, they will form a clearer picture of morality. At this point, their knowledge should include the following:

   - *Moral* and *morality* (as well as *ethics* and *ethical*) are words that describe action.

   - People need to learn morality.

   - Torah and *mitzvot* can help us become moral and ethical.

2. The tendency to abbreviate the name of the second tree that God created by calling it the Tree of Knowledge may mislead the students. This tree symbolizes moral knowledge and not factual information.

3. Adam's wife is called Eve because "she was the mother of all life." This is a play on the similarity between the words *Chava* חַוָּה, Eve, and *chaya* חַיָּה, living things.

Methodology

Introduction

1. In order to help the students learn the difference between right and wrong, ask them to list several actions that are wrong. Write the students' responses on the chalkboard. Then ask the students what makes these actions wrong. Do the same for actions that are right.

2. Have the students read the first three pages of Chapter 2, including the Torah text "The Garden of Eden." Review the highlights of the story by asking the students to outline its major events.

3. Have the students read and complete "Stories and Symbols" on pages 13 and 14. You may choose to invite questions and review the activities for clarification. Prepare a slide show, display, or collection of cards showing a variety of symbols (e.g., a lion, a hawk, a dove, an elephant, a donkey, a Star of David, a crucifix, a musical notation, a universal safety sign, etc.). Ask the students to explain the meaning of each symbol. Remind the students that the lion symbol used in this book, which indicates a Torah text, is a symbol for the Jewish people.

The person is
_____sleeping_____.

The person is
__in love_____.

The person is
___thinking of a new idea___.

The flame on the right can also be a symbol.
List as many meanings as you can for this symbol.

Possible answers include: anger, wisdom, passion, destruction, and creation.

4. Have each student complete the activities that appear on page 15. As a class, have the students list all the ways in which a tree can be a symbol. The students should then share their interpretations of the symbols that appear on the bottom of page 15. As a class, have the students reread the Torah text and then have each student write down his or her interpretation of the Garden of Eden, the Tree of Life, and the Tree of Knowledge of Good and Bad. Have the students share their responses.

In Chapter 1 you learned that the Tree of Life may be a symbol for the Torah. What else can a tree symbolize?

Possible answers include: new life, growing up, and giving.

Garden of Eden

Possible answers include: perfection, paradise, hope, birth, and childhood.

Tree of Life

Possible answers include: living forever and heaven.

Tree of Knowledge of Good and Bad

Possible answers include: decision making and the good and bad in each of us.

5. Have the students complete "Knowing Right and Wrong," which appears on page 16.

What Adam Did Wrong:	What Eve Did Wrong:
He took the fruit from Eve and ate it even though God told him not to.	She took and ate the forbidden fruit from the Tree of Knowledge of Good and Bad.

6. Have the students read the Torah text "Cain and Abel" on page 17. Then have them complete "The First Murder," which appears on page 18. Have the students act out and discuss their dialogues.

7. Have the students stage a trial in which the three defendants are Adam, Eve, and the snake. Have the students present the crimes that each of these defendants is alleged to have committed and then determine whether each one is responsible.

Closure

8. Have the students compare the two stories of Creation in Chapters 1 and 2 of the textbook. Ask: "What are the differences between the Torah texts in Chapters 1 and 2?" Tell the students to compare and contrast the two stories.

Enrichment Activity

Have the students read and discuss other origin and creation stories. Include stories like Rudyard Kipling's *Just So Stories* (New York: Doubleday, 1972). Plaut's *The Torah: A Modern Commentary* presents alternative Near Eastern creation stories on pages 24 and 32. See also Virginia Hamilton's *In The Beginning: Creation Stories from Around the World* (New York: Harcourt Brace Jovanovich, 1988).

Noah and the Flood

Chapter Summary

The story of Noah is the sequel to the stories of Creation. God's disappointment with human misconduct is a counterpoint to "And God saw that it was good." In this chapter we introduce the terms *tzadik* and *brit* and the Jewish affirmation of life in this world, *olam hazeh*.

Objectives

* Associate our own disappointment in projects we have undertaken that have failed with God's disappointment in human acts of immorality.

* Define the word *righteous* as doing the right thing and being a good, kind, and fair person.

* Define *brit* as an agreement between two people or two parties, which includes agreements between God and groups of people.

* Associate the terms *pikuach nefesh* and *tza'ar ba'alei chayim* with Judaism's teaching of respect for and the importance of preserving life.

Major Themes

- God wants people to behave in a righteous manner by acting with kindness and fairness toward one another.

- Just as we are sometimes disappointed when our projects don't turn out as we hope, God is disappointed when people behave immorally.

- Rules can help us to understand the difference between right and wrong so that we can know and choose to behave in a right way.

- Just as we can have an agreement, a *brit*, with a parent, a teacher, or a friend, we can make agreements with or promises to God.

Key Terms

Tzedakah צְדָקָה	"Rightness" or "Righteousness." Acting fairly, in the same way that we would want others to act toward us. *Tzedakah* includes providing money, food, and job-training assistance to the poor.
Tzadik צַדִּיק	A "righteous person." One whose good deeds help many.
Brit בְּרִית	A "covenant" or "contract." An agreement between two parties.
Chai חַי	"Living." From the word *chaim*, which means "life."

Background for the Teacher

1. Review the importance of *mitzvot*. Although the students are not likely at first to admit that rules are necessary, help them see that rules insure fairness and safety for everyone.

2. Discuss the term *tzedakah*. Make sure that the students do not confuse *tzedakah* with charity. Explain that charity is helping others out of kindness, whereas *tzedakah* is helping others because doing so is commanded by God.

3. Noah's ark was not a boat. It was a giant watertight box that was not equipped for navigation or piloting. It was called an ark—*aron* in Hebrew—because it was shaped like a box.

Methodology

Introduction

1. Ask each student to write about or discuss a creative project (e.g., building a model, making an artistic creation, etc.) that he or she is proud of. Have the students describe their projects and the steps that went into creating them. Ask the students whether creative endeavors always go smoothly. Have them discuss the kinds of obstacles that one can encounter. Close the discussion by explaining that in Chapter 3, we will read that God was disappointed with humanity and wanted to create the world anew. As the students read the chapter, ask them to pay special attention to the reasons for God's disappointment and God's plan for starting over.

2. Have the students read page 19 of Chapter 3, "Noah and the Flood."

3. Write the word *right* on the chalkboard. Ask the students to provide definitions of this word. Possible answers include "correct," "straight," "good," and "right-handed." Then write the word *brit* on the chalkboard. Explain that this word means "promise," "agreement," or "contract." Have the students read the Torah text "The Flood" on pages 20 and 21.

4. After the students have read and completed "Noah and His World," which appears on pages 22 and 23, have them share their responses with the class. Ask the students: "How did Noah walk with God?"

5. Have the students read and complete "The Rainbow" on pages 23 and 24. Have the students share their insights on what a *brit* is and what the specific terms of this particular *brit* include.

The Rainbow
1. __Be fruitful and multiply.__
2. __Be responsible for the animals.__
3. __Do not eat live animals; do not eat blood.__
4. __Be responsible for other people.__
5. __Do not kill other people.__
6. __Know that people are created in God's image.__

Closure

6. Have the class write a contract—a *brit*—that will serve as a behavioral and academic agreement between the students and the teacher. Make sure that the writing process is democratic and that the needs of both parties are met. Have all the parties sign a written version of the *brit* and post it on a classroom wall.

Enrichment Activities

1. Have the students design, build, or draw an ark based on a close reading of the description of the ark in the Torah. (For blueprint details of the ark, have the students read Genesis 6:14-16.)

2. Take the class to a zoo or an animal reserve. Identify the animals that Noah took aboard the ark. Tell the students the Hebrew names for the animals. Determine which animals are native to the Middle East. Observe those species that are endangered. Discuss the importance of protecting such endangered animals from extinction. Use Noah's preservation of the animals as a model for modern wildlife preservation efforts. Research the animal protection efforts of such organizations as The Society for the Protection of Nature in Israel, Greenpeace, the ASPCA, the Sierra Club, the Audubon Society, etc.

Abraham's New Direction

Chapter Summary

This chapter introduces Abraham and Sarah. Abraham stood firm in his belief in one God. He was a diplomat, an advocate of justice, and an example to those who "go forth" alone and begin anew. Abraham and Sarah are our familial and ideological progenitors. The activities in this chapter help the students to explore their feelings about their own individuality and to identify with Abraham and Sarah.

Objectives

- List ways in which one can assert one's Jewish identity.
- Analyze selections from Jewish literature, including the *Tanach*, that contain instances in which wise choices are made.
- Identify oneself as a member of the Jewish people.

Major Themes

- Being Jewish means being part of a family or people.
- Throughout our lives we, like Abraham and Sarah, face new journeys and challenges that are sometimes scary but always result in personal growth.
- Judaism admires independent thinking and respects sincere differences of opinion.

Key Terms

Ancestors אָבוֹת	This word, which means "one who goes before" in English, refers to any or all parents, grandparents, great-grandparents, etc.
Midrash מִדְרָשׁ	This word is derived from the Hebrew root meaning to "inquire, study, investigate." Rabbinic commentary on the Bible, which often employs stories, parables, and legends.
Idols אֱלִילִים	Representations or symbols of objects of worship. False gods.
Hebrew עִבְרִי	*Ivree*: a member of an ancient wandering Semitic people to which Abraham belonged.
עִבְרִית	*Ivreet*: the Hebrew language.
Brit Milah בְּרִית מִילָה	"Covenant of Circumcision." A ritual circumcision that involves the surgical removal of the foreskin from the end of the penis. Signifies a male's entrance into the covenant between God and the Jewish people.
Brit Chayim בְּרִית חַיִּים	"Covenant of Life." One of several rituals developed by Reform Judaism to signify a female's entrance into the covenant between God and the Jewish people.

Background for the Teacher

1. Because the legend of Abraham's breaking the idols appears very frequently in children's books that contain Jewish Bible stories, students tend to assume that it is in the Torah. Impress upon your students the importance of this story while emphasizing that it is a *midrash* and does not appear in the Bible.

2. This chapter includes readings from Genesis 12 and 17. Several important episodes occur between these chapters that were not included in the textbook because of lack of space. You may wish to read the following stories to your students or summarize them:

   - The Parting of Abraham and His Nephew Lot. (Genesis 13:7-12)

   - The Covenant between the Pieces. (Genesis 15)

   - The Birth of Abraham's Son Ishmael by Abraham's Concubine, Hagar. (Genesis 16)

3. Abraham and Sarah play an important role in the Jewish consciousness. Since they are considered our original Jewish mother and father, they render the Jewish people part of one family. This idea so pervades Jewish life that when a person converts to Judaism, he or she is often given the name Son or Daughter of Abraham and Sarah.

4. Judaism's teachings include respect for foreigners. Abraham and Moses, two of our greatest heroes, were both considered foreigners in the places in which they lived and worked. Because of their foreign status, they were especially sensitive to the plight of the stranger. As strangers in

a strange land, they valued hospitality highly. Hospitality continues to be an important value in Judaism.

Here are a few examples from the Bible in which a major figure refers to himself or herself as a foreigner. Abraham called himself a *ger toshav*, "resident stranger," when he sought to buy burial land. Moses named his son Gershom, saying, *Ger hayiti be'eretz nachriyah*, "I have been a stranger in a strange land." Ruth, the great-grandmother of King David, was also a stranger from the foreign land of Moab.

Methodology

Introduction

1. Read the introduction to Chapter 4, "Abraham's New Direction," on page 25. Begin a discussion about people who have experimented with new ideas. Ask: "How did such individuals implement their new ideas? What characteristics must an individual who tries out new ideas possess? What kind of obstacles might he or she encounter?"

Learning Activities

2. Have the students read the *midrash* "Abraham and the Idols" on page 26. Help the students generate a list of modern forms of idol worship.

3. Have the students read and complete "Being Different" on page 27. Direct the students to form pairs and have each pair of students share their answers with each other. Ask each student in the class to list three traits that distinguishes him or her from others in the class. Have each student choose one or more of these characteristics and proclaim, "I am *kadosh*, 'holy, special,' because...."

> Shem's son is named ___Arpachshad___.
>
> Shem's grandson is named ___Shelah___.
>
> Nahor's son is named ___Terah___.
>
> Terah's son is named ___Abraham___.

4. Have the students read and complete the activities for "The Family of Abraham" on pages 28 and 29. The chart on page 29 counts 20 generations.

5. Have the students read the Torah text "Go Forth" on page 30. Then have the students complete the activities for "Finding New Directions" on page 31. Begin a discussion of the experience of finding oneself in a new situation. For example, ask the students: "How is attending a new school or synagogue or moving to a new neighborhood akin to being a stranger?" Invite the students to share their own experiences.

Finding New Directions

In this Torah text God made a *brit* with Abraham. Put a check [✔] next to the promises that God made to Abraham.

✔ large family   ✔ power
✔ blessings   ✔ land to Abraham's descendants
✔ wealth   ✔ leadership of an important nation

What does God ask Abraham to promise in return? Why does God ask this?

<u>God asks Abraham to leave his native land. God asks this to make</u>

<u>sure that Abraham will be faithful to God.</u>

6. Read the Torah text "The Father of Many Nations" on page 32. Discuss the text, drawing particular attention to the terms of the *brit* between Abraham and God. Include the following:

   a. Avram's name will be changed to Abraham.

   b. Abraham will have many descendants, including kings.

   c. Abraham and his descendants will receive the land of Canaan.

   d. Abraham and his descendants are to observe the *mitzvah* of circumcision as a symbol of the *brit*.

   e. Sarai's name will be changed to Sarah.

   f. Sarah will give birth to a son.

7. Have the students read "What's in a Name?" on the top of page 33. Ask them to share their names and nicknames, explaining, when possible, how they received those names. Have them look up the meaning of their names in a name dictionary and then have each student design a poster illustrating certain aspects of his or her name(s).

8. Have the students read "The Covenant" on page 33. Allow time for the students to share stories about how births are celebrated in their family.

Closure

9. As a closing activity, have the students read the *Avot* prayer. An English translation of this prayer can be found in *Gates of Prayer*, page 134. Have the students think about stories they've heard about their parents, grandparents, and great-grandparents. Then explain that in Judaism we have an ideal called *zehut avot*, "merit of ancestors," which teaches us that our lives are enriched by the lives and the good deeds of our parents, grandparents, and great-grandparents. Lead the students in a discussion of the past generation's positive traits and the good deeds that the students wish to continue in their own generation. Then reread the *Avot* prayer.

Enrichment Activities

1. Read *Molly's Pilgrim* by Barbara Cohen (New York: Lothrop, Lee & Shepard, 1983). Like Abraham, Molly was a stranger in a new land who asserted her presence as a true pilgrim.

2. Have the students develop and present a skit titled "Breaking Modern Idols," based on the *midrash* about Abraham that appears on page 26 of the textbook.

3. To help the students follow the travels of their ancestors, post a world map on a bulletin board. Have the students identify their family's cities of origin by putting colored pushpins in the correct places on the map. If class size allows, have each student attach a colored piece of yarn to the pins to show his or her family's pattern of settlement. Assign a different color to each student.

4. Invite a *mohel* or obstetrician/pediatrician to talk to the class about circumcision from a religious and/or clinical viewpoint.

The Testing of Abraham

Chapter Summary

In this chapter the students begin to examine revelation through two stories—Abraham's welcoming of the visitors and the *Akeda*, the "Binding" of Isaac.

The story of the *Akeda* is one of the most difficult and haunting narratives in the Torah. *Torah: The Growing Gift* focuses on the more positive lessons of this particular revelation rather than on the more negative aspects of tests of allegiance and parental abandonment.

Objectives

- Define *revelation* as the experience of seeing or hearing God and of learning from God through signs or the actions of others.

- Identify stories of revelation found in the *Tanach*, including the Torah.

- Define *sacrifice* as the giving of gifts to God.

Major Themes

- It is a *mitzvah* to welcome guests and strangers.

- An experience whereby a person or people see or perceive God is called a revelation. Sometimes God is revealed through the actions of others.

- God does not desire human sacrifice.

Key Terms

Revelation	From the Latin root meaning to "uncover," the word *reveal* means to show something or oneself in such a way that the observer learns something. The word *revelation* is most often used to describe experiences in which God is revealed to a person or people.
Hachnasat Orechim הַכְנָסַת אוֹרְחִים	The "welcoming of guests." The *mitzvah* of hospitality, as demonstrated by Abraham toward the three men.
Sacrifice עֲבוֹדָה, קוֹרְבָּן	From the Latin for "holy work." Identified with the Hebrew terms *avodah*, "service," and *korban*, "offering." The word *sacrifice* refers to gifts offered to God.
Malach מַלְאָךְ	An "angel" or "messenger."
Gemilut Chasadim גְמִילוּת חֲסָדִים	"Acts of loving-kindness."
Akeda עֲקֵדָה	"Binding," from the story in which Abraham "bound" or tied up Isaac as an offering to God.

Background for the Teacher

1. What is a sacrifice? While many details about ancient Israelite sacrifices are presented in Chapter 18, it is important to clear up any misconceptions about sacrifices from the start. For ancient people, offering sacrifices meant giving gifts of food to God or to many gods. For ancient Jews in particular, offering sacrifices also meant sharing family meals with God. When a family brought offerings to the Temple, a portion of the bread, fruit, or meat would often be burned on the altar while the family enjoyed a meal.

   Offering sacrifices was not a barbaric or inhumane act. Animals that were used in sacrifices were killed by trained priests who made certain that they inflicted the least possible pain on the animals. As mentioned above, most of the meat of the sacrificed animals was used as food for people, both for the families and the priests. Normally only the fat and other inedible portions of the sacrificed animals were burned in their entirety.

   Judaism teaches that human sacrifice is not an acceptable form of worship. Human life is held to be among the highest of Jewish values, taking precedence over all rituals.

2. God does not tempt human beings by playing grotesque games. The notion of a God who teases people into submission by challenging their loyalty is foreign to Judaism. Human sacrifice was an abhorrent idea to Judaism from the very beginning.

To make theological sense of the *Akeda*, one must remember that in Abraham's time, it was not unusual to think that gods desire human sacrifices. An ideological innovator like Abraham would naturally challenge such an assumption. Thus the *Akeda* is not about God's testing of Abraham but rather about Abraham's testing of God. Abraham is setting a new standard for the relationship between God and humanity.

3. Because of space constraints, two stories were not included in *Torah: The Growing Gift*. They are (1) The Destruction of Sodom and Gomorrah (Genesis 19) and (2) The Exile of Hagar and Ishmael (Genesis 21:9-21). You may wish to present these texts or a summary of them to your students.

Methodology

Introduction

1. Begin with a theological discussion that focuses on the ways in which people perceive God. You may wish to use the following sequence of questions as a guide. Ask the students:

   • How do you imagine God?

   • Does God have arms, legs, a mouth, and eyes?

   • What do we mean when we say that God is invisible but everywhere?

   • What do the biblical phrases "in God's eyes" and "the hands of God" mean?

   • How can someone see God?

   • Is seeing God similar to seeing anything else?

   Summarize or ask a student or group of students to summarize the discussion. Tell the students that in this chapter they will learn how God was seen by our patriarch Abraham.

Learning Activities

2. Have the students read the introduction to Chapter 5, "The Testing of Abraham," on page 34, as well as the Torah text "Revelation" on page 35. Then tell them to complete the activities on page 36. Discuss the meaning of revelation. Ask the students: "What are some of the ways in which we can encounter God?" Invite the students' speculation, as well as recountings of their personal experiences. Ask: "Can God appear to us through people? Nature? Inanimate objects? Actions? Feelings?"

How Do We "See" God?

Some people think God "appears" through acts of loving-kindness, *gemilut chasadim* גְּמִילוּת חֲסָדִים. Read the story again. How many kind acts performed by Abraham for the visitors can you find? Make a list of the acts in the box below.

> He ran to greet them.
> He invited them to rest.
> He brought them water.
> He gave them bread.
> He and Sarah prepared cakes, tender veal, cheese, and milk for them.
> He served them this food.

3. Provide the students with scissors and magazines and ask them to make posters that show how people experience God as Creator, Provider, Redeemer (i.e., Saver of Victims), Ruler, Healer, etc.

4. Have the students read and complete "The Revelation of the Akeda" on page 38. Ask for volunteers to share their answers.

The Revelation of the Akeda

1. Explain how God tested Abraham.

God asked Abraham to offer his son Isaac as a burnt offering.

2. Abraham's revelation in this Torah text is quite different from his revelation in the story of the three men. How does God appear to Abraham in the *Akeda* story?

God appears first as a voice and then as an angel.

3. What do you think that Abraham learned from his revelation in the *Akeda* story?

Abraham learned that God's test was not going to harm Isaac and that he could trust God to protect him and his descendants.

5. There is a *midrash* that begins with the following line from the Torah:

   On the third day Abraham looked up and saw the place from far away. (Genesis 22:4)

The *midrash* then continues. Abraham asked if Isaac saw the place. The boy said, "Yes, Father." Abraham then asked the two servants if they saw it. They answered, "We don't see anything but a mountain." Here the *midrash* returns to the Torah text:

Then Abraham said to the servants, "You stay here with the donkey. The boy and I will go and worship.... (Genesis 22:5)

Have the students discuss and/or act out the roles of the people in this *midrash*. Ask the students: "What did Abraham and Isaac see that the servants did not? What enabled Abraham and Isaac to see what they saw?"

Closure

6. As a creative writing exercise, have the students compose one or more diary entries retelling the events of the *Akeda* narrative from the point of view of Abraham, Isaac, the servants, the donkey, or the ram caught in a bush.

Enrichment Activities

1. Genesis 19 describes the story of the destruction of Sodom and Gomorrah. Class time permitting, develop and present a lesson based on this Torah text prior to beginning Chapter 6.

2. Have the students explore Sarah's role in the *Akeda* story.

From Generation to Generation

Chapter Summary

In this chapter stories from the Torah help the students to increase their understanding of life-cycle events. The courtship of Isaac and Rebecca shows how our values influence our choice of friends and mates. The deaths of Sarah and Abraham show how ancient Israelites responded to death in their family.

Objectives

- Recognize that kindness to others is an important criterion for selecting friends and mates.
- Identify matchmaking and marriage counseling as difficult endeavors that are highly valued in Judaism.
- Recognize death as a significant life-cycle stage, and identify the acts of burial and mourning as *mitzvot*.
- Read stories about ancient Jewish family life in order to gain insights into one's own family life.

Major Themes

- If one of our criteria for choosing our friends is their kindness, we can be fairly certain that the friends we choose will be true friends.

- Kindness to our fellow human beings, *gemilut chasadim*, and kindness to animals, *tza'ar ba'alei chayim*, are important Jewish values.

- Burial and mourning rituals after a family member's death follow specific Jewish customs that are considered a vital part of life.

Key Terms

Prayer תְּפִלָּה	A form of individual or private worship in which the worshiper reflects and/or asks for support from God. The Hebrew word *tefilah* means "self-examination."
Mourning אֲבֵלוּת	A period of time during which signs of grief are shown in response to the death of a loved one.

Background for the Teacher

1. Burial and Mourning. Although specific details are not provided, the Torah text hints at certain *mitzvot* that pertain to burial and mourning. Judaism teaches that it is a *mitzvah* to bury the dead with dignity and respect. The *mitzvah* of burying the dead is the responsibility of the deceased's spouse or children. It is a *mitzvah* for all who are able to do so to attend a funeral service. See *Gates of Mitzvah*, edited by Simeon J. Maslin (New York: CCAR, 1979, pages 54 to 56) for a more detailed Reform explanation of these observances.

   Grieving and mourning are not the same thing. Grieving is an emotion, whereas mourning consists of a set of behaviors. Even though mourning for the dead is a *mitzvah* for the whole community, grief is considered to be a very personal emotion.

   The Torah text does not tell us how long Abraham mourned for Sarah. Jewish tradition, however, prescribes several periods of mourning. The most intense period is *shivah*, the seven days following the funeral, during which family members remain at home, avoid ordinary pursuits, and pray daily. *Shivah* is followed by *sheloshim*, the thirty-day period that includes *shivah*, after which normal life resumes. For those mourning for a parent, the mourning period is extended to twelve months. For eleven months they recite the *Mourner's Kaddish* at every service.

2. Betrothal and Marriage. The story of the servant who was sent to seek a wife for Isaac reveals certain interesting practices. First, Rebecca was chosen by Abraham's servant rather than by Isaac. Second, the servant took with him a gift of ten camels. Third, Rebecca was chosen from among Abraham's relatives.

   Until relatively recently, marriages were often arranged by parents. In part this was due to the fact that the bride and groom were often young—as young as twelve—and considered too young to make a lifelong decision without their parents' guidance. In addition, the marriage was not only between the bride and groom but also between their two families. Marriage between cousins was permitted. In fact, parents usually preferred that their children married someone from their clan or tribe.

   Before becoming engaged to a woman, a man normally had to pay a bride-price to the girl's father. This exchange took the form of either money or property. In Isaac's case the ten camels were used as a bride-price.

3. The servant sent by Abraham to find a wife for Isaac is never identified by name. Jewish tradition commonly identifies that servant as Eliezer, the servant named in Genesis 15:2.

4. The Well Motif. The story of the servant's meeting Rebecca is the first of several stories in the Torah that link courtship with wells of water. In each case the participants—in this case by proxy—meet at a well. An act of kindness or heroism by one of the participants provides water, and the betrothal occurs.

Methodology

Introduction

1. Ask the students to cite examples of life-cycle events. Generate a list on the chalkboard that includes birth, bar/bat mitzvah, marriage, divorce, and death. Inform the students that in this lesson they will be reading selections from Torah texts that teach about death and marriage.

Learning Activities

2. Explain to the students that it is a *mitzvah* to participate in a marriage celebration or a burial ceremony. Ask the students if any of them have recently participated in one of these life-cycle events. Invite several students to describe briefly the event that they attended.

3. Have the students read "The Death of Sarah" on page 40. Discuss the story with the students. You might wish to use the following discussion questions:

   - How do people feel when a loved one dies?

   - What are some of the ways in which a person might act when he or she learns about the death of a loved one?

   - Why do people feel or act the way they do after the death of a loved one?

   - What can people do to make mourning easier for themselves or others?

   - Why was burying Sarah important to Abraham?

   - Why did Abraham say, "I am a stranger living among you" before he asked to buy a burial site for Sarah?

   - Why is it a *mitzvah* to help bury the dead?

4. Have the students read and complete "A Wife for Isaac" on pages 41 and 42.

A Wife for Isaac: A Closer Look

In biblical times parents usually arranged the marriage of their children. Often people would marry cousins, distant relatives, or the son or daughter of family friends.

When Abraham's servant arrived in the city of Nachor, he prayed to God. Read over the part of the Torah text in which the servant prayed. What was he praying for?

He was praying for good fortune and a wife for Isaac.

The servant asked for a sign to help him recognize the right woman for Isaac. What was the sign?

He asked that a woman offer water for his camels.

Why do you think the servant chose that sign to recognize Isaac's future bride?

He was looking for a kind woman.

5	**3**	**1**	**8**
Rebecca offers water to the servant.	Rebecca comes to the well to draw water.	The servant takes ten camels and heads for Nahor.	The servant thanks God for finding a wife for Isaac.
2	**7**	**6**	**4**
The servant stops at a well and prays for help.	Rebecca offers to let the servant stay at her father's house.	Rebecca draws water for the servant's camels.	The servant asks Rebecca for a sip of water.

Look again at the description of the scenes above. Remember that the things people do show what kind of people they are. What kind of person was Rebecca? Explain your answer.

Rebecca was kind and generous. She was caring and liked giving to others.

5. Discuss the criteria for selecting a friend. Ask the students: "What are the characteristics of a good friend? What are the characteristics of a successful friendship?" Have the students compare various ways of choosing friends.

6. Have the students read "The Generation of Isaac" on page 43. Examine with them the chronology of the following four events: the Binding of Isaac, the death of Sarah, the marriage of Isaac and Rebecca, and the death of Abraham. Ask: "How is each event related to the preceding one?"

7. Have the students list and discuss each of the *mitzvot* performed in the Torah texts, including *hachnasat orechim*—the "welcoming of guests"—*tza'ar ba'alei chayim*—"kindness to animals"—burial, and mourning.

Closure

8. Have the students rewrite the story of Rebecca at the well as a play and perform it in class. Produce a videotape of the presentation. Stage performances for students in other grades.

Enrichment Activities

1. Have the students listen to the songs "Matchmaker, Matchmaker" and "Do You Love Me?" from *Fiddler on the Roof*, or show them the appropriate scenes from the film. Discuss the similarities and differences between the marriage practices and romantic attitudes depicted in the film and the Torah text, as well as those we encounter today.

2. Values Clarification Exercise: Four Corners. Make four signs, each of which lists a reason to marry. Include Love, Common Tastes, Same Religion, and, as a fourth, consider Same Social Class, Physical Attraction, or Arranged by Parents. The students must select an answer in reply to the question "Which single factor is the most important in making a good marriage?" Have the students go to one of four corners of the room, based on their answer. Have the students in each corner discuss their choice and then share/discuss/debate the issue with the entire class.

3. Invite a rabbi or marriage counselor from the synagogue to visit the class as a guest speaker and answer questions about the makings of a good marriage.

4. Invite a rabbi or a member of a *Chevrah Kadisha*, Burial Society, to visit the class as a guest speaker and answer questions about death, burial, and coping with grief.

Twins

Chapter Summary

In this classic story of sibling rivalry and deception, we learn that Jacob, the father of the nation of Israel, was once a selfish opportunist, a heel. We follow his moral development in the next few chapters.

Objectives

- Identify what constitutes selfish and thoughtless acts.

- Explore the relationship between siblings and the issue of sibling rivalry.

- Identify blessings as a vital part of Jewish life.

- Explore stories about Jewish family life in order to gain insights into one's own family life.

Major Themes

- Sibling rivalry—competition among brothers and sisters—is common and sometimes hurtful.

- We can enrich our life and the lives of family members through blessings.

Key Terms

Birthright

בְּכוֹרָה

From the Hebrew for *bechor*, "firstborn." In the Near East of biblical times, the birthright was generally a double portion of inheritance that the eldest male child was to receive after the death of the father. While custom favored the firstborn son, the Torah does not say that God and/or history showed such favoritism. Neither Isaac, Jacob, Judah, nor Joseph was the firstborn.

Blessing

בְּרָכָה

A blessing, *berachah*, is a specific type of prayer that praises the attributes of God or God's gifts to humankind. In the story of Esau and Jacob, Isaac's blessing is desired because it is the final proclamation on the future of the blessed one. This type of blessing apparently had great significance in ancient Israel.

Background for the Teacher

1. Names. In the Torah people's names often involve wordplay. Jacob, *Ya'akov*, is a pun on heel, *akev*. The name Esau appears to be related to *se'ar*, "hair."

   The Torah also calls attention to Esau's other name, *Edom*, which is a triple-entendre on (1) the red stew, *ha'adom ha'adom*, most likely a lentil soup that Esau wanted to eat (*adom* means "red"); (2) Esau's ruddiness; and (3) Esau's association with the Edomites, a neighboring nation frequently at odds with Israel. The two brothers were also frequently in conflict.

2. Readers of the Torah text often confuse the birthright with the blessing. Note that the Hebrew names for birthright and blessing are the same, בְּכוֹרָה and בְּרָכָה, except for an inversion of the middle two letters.

3. None of the people in this narrative is blameless. In particular, it is important that the students recognize that Jacob wants to get ahead and doesn't care if someone else suffers in the process. It is crucial, however, that the students also see Jacob as being redeemable. Tell the students that in the chapters that follow, they will see moral growth on Jacob's part that parallels the change in Joseph in Chapter 11.

4. The Torah does not condone deception, even though a deception established Jacob's legacy. Jacob pays a heavy price for his dishonesty. Later in Jacob's life his sons deceive him and tell him that his beloved son Joseph is dead. Just as Jacob deceived his own father, so, too, Jacob's sons trick him. Whenever deception or dishonesty occurs, whether it be in the classroom, the family, or the workplace, *tzedek*, "fairness," is abandoned.

Methodology

Introduction

1. Have each student draw a picture or diagram of his or her family, i.e., the people—including parents and siblings—with whom the student lives most of the time.

Learning Activities

2. Have the students look at their finished picture (above) and think about whether there are particular roles, relationships, or alliances in their family. Have them ask themselves the following: Are there two family members who frequently argue? Are there two family members who typically cooperate with each other more than with other family members? Who makes the decisions about matters within the house? Who makes the decisions about matters outside the house?

   Sum up this activity by explaining that in this lesson the students will be examining the relationships among the members of one family in the Torah. The students may be surprised to learn that the predominant decision maker in the household of Isaac and Rebecca was Rebecca.

3. Have the students read the Torah text "The Birth of Esau and Jacob" on page 46 and complete the activity "All in the Family" on the same page. Introduce the concept of foreshadowing. Explain that the Torah often uses foreshadowing to give the reader a glimpse of what will happen later. Have the students reread the above Torah text aloud. Ask them to speculate on what events are being foreshadowed.

All in the Family

Why do you think that Isaac and Rebecca wanted children?

They wanted children to love and to continue the line of Abraham.

When Esau was about to be born, Jacob tried to pull him back. He grabbed his brother's heel because he wanted to be the older one. Why do you think that Jacob wanted to be the firstborn?

He wanted the inheritance and privileges of the firstborn.

4. Have the students read "Esau Sells His Birthright" on page 47. Ask them to summarize the events in this Torah text. You might wish to use the following questions and topics to stimulate discussion:

   • Have any of the predictions that were foreshadowed in the previous Torah text been realized?

   • What is a birthright? (You might need to provide some background here. See Key Terms, above.)

   • Has Jacob done anything immoral?

   • Has Esau done anything immoral?

5. Have the students read the Torah text "The Trick and the Blessing" on pages 48 and 49. Discuss the meaning of "blessing," *berachah*. You might wish to use the following questions to stimulate discussion:

   • How is a blessing different from a birthright?

   • Are there any parallels in modern culture for birthrights and blessings?

   • Has Isaac done anything immoral?

   • Has Jacob done anything immoral?

   • Has Rebecca done anything immoral?

6. Have the students read and complete "Torah Detective" on pages 50 and 51. A class discussion of this activity may reveal a variety of comments about ethical conduct. The purpose here is to identify the moral shortcomings and to deepen understanding of the characters involved in the Torah text.

7. Have the students share the blessing they wrote for the textbook activity that appears on page 52.

Closure

8. Suggest that the students reenact the story of the deception of Isaac as a skit. Then have them stage a series of courtroom trials. Jacob should be charged with fraud and theft. Rebecca should be tried for aiding and abetting theft and fraud. Isaac may be tried for giving only one blessing when he had two sons. Assign roles for all the participants in the narrative and appoint a judge, a jury, a defense team, and prosecuting attorneys.

Enrichment Activities

1. Have the students look up the meaning of their Hebrew or English name(s) in a dictionary of names and then write whether their character corresponds to that meaning.

2. Use the topics of birthright and blessing to teach the students about living wills and traditional Jewish blessings.

Jacob Leaves Home

Chapter Summary

In this chapter we watch Jacob grow and mature. The students will read about Jacob's dream of the ladder—or stairway—his courtship of Rachel, and his dealings with Laban. Dreams and dream interpretation are also explored.

Objectives

- Interpret Jacob's dream of the ladder as symbolizing key factors in his life, e.g., change, growth, God's presence, tension, etc.

- Identify irony in the fact that Jacob's act of kindness toward Rachel at the well begets Laban's trickery.

- Associate the word *miracle* with turning points in the Bible.

Major Themes

- The contents of dreams are often symbolic.

- In the Bible the water well often serves as a symbol for romantic love.

- Good deeds do not immediately reap positive results.

Key Term

Sulam
סֻלָּם

A Hebrew word of indeterminate meaning. Something used for going up and down, i.e., a ladder or a stairway.

Background for the Teacher

1. Before attempting to interpret Jacob's dream, the students should bear in mind the events that immediately preceded the dream. After violent threats made by his brother, Jacob was forced to move, leaving his home and his parents, possibly forever.

2. Angels. Contrary to common assumption, Judaism contains many references to angels. The Hebrew word for angel, *malach*, means "messenger" and refers to entities used by God to perform various duties. While angels are given both animal and human form in the Torah, most commentators suggest that angels are symbolic. For other appearances of angels in the Torah, see Genesis 18:1-22, 19:1-26, 21:17, 22:11, 31:11-13; Exodus 3:2, 23:20-24; and Numbers 20:16. See also Plaut, *The Torah: A Modern Commentary*, page 124.

3. Betrothal and Marriage. In this chapter Jacob falls in love with his cousin Rachel and marries both Rachel and her sister Leah. As was pointed out in the Background for the Teacher for Chapter 6 on page 32 of this guide, people in the ancient Near East often married members of their own clan. A man was permitted to have more than one wife at a time although monogamy was preferred and marriage to two sisters was very unusual.

    A gift was normally paid to the father of the bride before a man became engaged to a woman. In Isaac's case ten camels were used as the bride-price. Since Jacob came to Laban empty-handed, seven years of service became the bride-price for each wife.

4. Because of space constraints, the story of the speckled sheep and Jacob's departure from Haran (Genesis 30:25-31:55) is not included in *Torah: The Growing Gift*. You may wish to present this text or a summary of it to your students.

Methodology

Introduction

1. Have the students draw a picture about a change that they have experienced. Possible subjects include a move, a first time at sleepaway camp, or any new experience that involved change and responsibility. Ask each student to tell how the experience affected his or her life.

2. Ask the students to think about the character of Jacob, focusing on his flaws. Tell them that in this lesson they will read about how Jacob began to mature so that he eventually became a kind and responsible person. They will also read about a mystical dream Jacob had that helped him begin making changes in his life.

3. Have the students read the Torah text "The Journey" on page 54. Pause to allow time for questions. Answer the students' questions but avoid any interpretation of the dream or its elements, explaining that the students will answer these questions themselves when they reach the end of the chapter.

4. Have the students read and complete "What Are Dreams?" on page 55. The students are likely to want to share their dream experiences. Allow time for a brief discussion.

5. Have the students read and complete the first activity on page 56. Then assign the parts of narrator, God, and Jacob to three students and have them read aloud the Torah text on page 54. Have the class complete the second activity on page 56.

Jacob's Ladder

A. SYMBOLS

1. ___stone (pillow)___
2. ___angels___
3. ___ladder___
4. ___sky___

B. MEANING

1. ___hardship, homelessness___
2. ___heaven, purity___
3. ___path to God, gateway to heaven___
4. ___God's presence___

6. Discuss the meaning of Jacob's dream. You might wish to use the following questions to stimulate discussion:

   - What are the possible functions and roles of the ladder and the angels in Jacob's dream?

   - What is the significance of the fact that angels were ascending and descending the ladder?

   - What promises did God make in the dream? Are these fair promises for God to make?

   - What might God ask of Jacob in exchange?

7. Have the students complete the activity "Laban's Trick" on page 59. You might wish to use the following questions to stimulate discussion:

   - How did Jacob's action at the well compare with his behavior until then?

   - What motivated Jacob's behavior?

   - Why did Laban act as he did? What kind of a person was he?

Closure

8. Have the students draw Jacob's dream, using crayons, pastels, paint, clay, or any other medium.

Enrichment Activities

1. Have the students look for books on Jewish art in the library of your temple. Help them locate and examine works of art that depict Jacob's dream. Have them try to detect common patterns in the art and identify the elements that were added by individual artists.

2. Have the students read various biblical stories and/or passages that involve angels intervening in human affairs (see page 41 of this guide). Ask: "What do these stories and/or passages have in common?" Have the students compare and contrast the images in the stories and/or passages with common perceptions of angels. For further study have the students compare the angels in these stories and/or passages with those found in Isaiah 6:2 and Ezekiel 1.

Jacob Wrestles

Chapter Summary

The strange wrestling match that takes place in this chapter symbolizes the inner struggles that all humans experience. Various explanations of this encounter will be explored. The name Israel will be discussed. This event marks the climax of Jacob's moral evolution.

Objectives

- List and explain the four steps of *teshuvah*.

- Identify the name Israel with Jacob and the Jewish people.

Major Themes

- Correcting past errors, *teshuvah*, is a difficult process that can be likened to wrestling.

- Jews are a struggling people. We "wrestle" with the world, with ourselves, with each other, and with God.

Key Terms

Teshuvah תְּשׁוּבָה	Literally a "turning" or "repenting." The process of changing one's ways toward a new, more positive direction. A turning away from the mistakes of the past to new possibilities in the future.
Selichah סְלִיחָה	"Pardon." The process of asking for or granting forgiveness.
Israel יִשְׂרָאֵל	The Jewish people. Also the name given to Jacob because he struggled with God and survived.

Background for the Teacher

1. Before the students read and attempt to understand Jacob's experience wrestling with the man throughout the night, have them recall the events that immediately preceded this event, i.e., Jacob's journey home and his planned reunion with his brother. Help the students see that the dream incident reflects some of Jacob's worries and hopes for his impending homecoming and meeting with Esau.

2. There is no single interpretation for the revelation that Jacob has as a result of his wrestling with the "man." While commentators almost universally refer to Jacob's opponent as an angel, that fact is not at all clear from the text. Scholars have identified the "man" as either God, Esau, one of Esau's soldiers, Esau's guardian angel, the spirit of the river, a vampire, a local angel, and even Jacob's own subconscious. Which interpretation your students choose is not important. Just be certain that they pick an interpretation they can defend—one that offers insight into the narrative.

3. Names continue to be filled with significance in the stories about Jacob. Jacob is called Israel, we are told, because he "wrestled with God and with people, and… survived." *Yisrael* may come from the root *sarah*, to "struggle" or "wrestle," and the suffix *El*, God. Taken together, the name means "God wrestler" or "God's wrestler."

   There is also a wordplay on the name Jacob in this story. The site of the wrestling match is the Jabbok River and the Hebrew word used in the Torah for "wrestling" is *ye'avek*.

Methodology

Introduction

1. The following role-play activity will introduce the students to the subject of reconciliation. Invite two students to enact the first situation as though it were real life. Then ask the discussion questions below. Repeat the activity with two new students playing the roles. Then go on to the second situation and repeat it.

   SITUATION 1   Your parents have discovered a game cartridge in your room that doesn't belong to you. When they confront you, you admit that you took it from Person B without asking. Your parents suggest that you apologize to Person B for taking the game.

SITUATION 2   During class Person A answered a teacher's question incorrectly. Without thinking, Person B made a joke about Person A and his or her answer. Too late, Person B saw that Person A was already extremely embarrassed and the comment had only made the matter worse. After class, A and B find themselves face-to-face.

Ask the participants the following questions:

- What were you thinking while you were playing your role?

- What feelings did you experience? Why do you think you were feeling that way?

- What choices did you make while playing your role? What choices did you reject?

- Did the feelings that you had before the confrontation change after it? Explain.

Learning Activities

2. Have the students read and complete the activities for "Jacob Goes Home" on page 61 and "Making Changes: Teshuvah" on page 62. Then have a class member read the Torah text on the left column of page 63 aloud, up to "Jacob was left alone." You may wish to use the following questions to stimulate discussion:

- What did Jacob do to prepare for his meeting with Esau?

- Why did he do these things?

- Why was Jacob afraid?

- Why did he send gifts?

- Was it right or wrong for Jacob to send gifts to Esau?

- How else could Jacob have fulfilled the same goal?

3. As a class, read the rest of "Jacob Becomes Israel" on pages 63 and 64. Have the students complete "Who Wrestled with Jacob?" on page 65. Divide the students into groups of three. Instruct them to discuss, explore, and present a unique theory about whom or what Jacob fought.

   Remind the students that when the word *Israel* appears in the Torah or a prayer book, it refers to the Jewish people. Invite the students to share their thoughts on what being a God wrestler means.

Who Wrestled with Jacob?

The mystery of this Torah text is, Who wrestled with Jacob? In the space below write your opinion about who—or what—wrestled with Jacob that night.

Possible answers include: an angel, Jacob's conscience, a demon.

4. Have the students read and complete the answers for "Selichah: Esau and Jacob Are Reunited" on page 65. Note that the text does not use the term *apology* or the phrase *I'm sorry*. Facilitate a class discussion about apologetic actions and the words *I apologize*. Ask the students to debate whether Jacob did show sincere *selichah*. The third question may not be applicable if a student chose the answer No for the first and second questions. Review and discuss this activity as a class. Ask the students: "Did Jacob complete the steps for *teshuvah*?"

Selichah: Esau and Jacob Are Reunited

The story of Jacob and Esau raises an important question: Did Jacob follow the four steps of *teshuvah* that are listed on page 62? To decide, answer the following questions by checking **Yes** or **No**.

Did Jacob apologize to Esau?	☑ Yes	☐ No
Did Jacob ask for *selichah*?	☑ Yes	☐ No
Did Esau accept Jacob's apology?	☑ Yes	☐ No
Did Jacob right his wrong?	☑ Yes	☐ No
Did Jacob pray and ask for *selichah* from God?	☑ Yes	☐ No
As far as you know, did Jacob repeat any of his wrong actions or deeds?	☐ Yes	☑ No
Do you think that Jacob deserved to be forgiven?	☑ Yes	☐ No

Closure

5. Use one or both of the following activities to conclude the lesson:

   • Have the students act out the story of the Torah text "Jacob Becomes Israel." Follow up with a discussion. Ask the students to examine whether Jacob accomplished *teshuvah*.

   • Have the students rewrite the skit above to include all four steps of *teshuvah*.

Enrichment Activities

1. Suggest to the students that since all Jewish people are Israel, we are all God wrestlers. Explore with the class possible interpretations and ramifications of this statement. Ask the students: "In what ways do Jews wrestle with God?"

2. Have the students write short stories about wrestling matches they have had with themselves, during which they worked out their own struggles.

3. Have the students draw the story of Jacob's wrestling match.

4. Have the students work in small groups to write a detective story in which a private eye is hired to solve the mystery of who wrestled with Jacob. Tell them to include interviews, a visit to the scene of the event, an exploration of motives, etc.

Jacob's Children

Chapter Summary

This is the first of two chapters about Joseph. Chapter 10 is also about dreams, jealousy, and exile. Like the young Jacob, Joseph was a pampered and arrogant young man who invoked the wrath of his brothers and was made to suffer. Chapter 11 tells about Joseph's moral and social climb from slavery, which parallels his father's sojourn in Haran.

Objectives

* Identify the thirteen children of Jacob and their respective mothers.

* Recall stories about ancient Jewish families in order to gain insights into one's own family.

- Identify arrogance and favoritism as obstacles to the development of positive personal relationships.

Major Themes

- Sibling rivalry led to a major crisis in Jacob's childhood. However, as an adult, he was unable to foresee that the same familial conflict would break up his own family. In fact, Jacob planted the seed of sibling rivalry in his own children's relationships.

- In this chapter Joseph is portrayed as a colorful dreamer. In the next chapter he proves himself to be a skilled dream interpreter.

Key Term

Keriah

קְרִיעָה

The act of tearing or rending one's garment as a sign of grief in response to the news of the death of an immediate family member. In ancient times mourners tore their own garment. Today mourners will often cut a black ribbon or piece of cloth as a sign of grief.

Background for the Teacher

Two stories found within the Joseph story are not included in *Torah: The Growing Gift* because of space constraints as well as the maturity of their subject matter. You may wish to present these stories in text or summary form to your students. These stories are The Rape of Dinah (Genesis 34) and Judah and Tamar (Genesis 38).

Methodology

Introduction

1. Begin by informing the students that a climactic point in the Book of Genesis occurs in the next two chapters of *Torah: The Growing Gift*. The narrative of Joseph is the longest story in Genesis. It consists of thirteen chapters and contains many of the themes presented earlier in the Torah—dreams, sibling rivalry, surviving difficult tests, standing by one's principles, and acting righteously.

Learning Activities

2. Have the students read aloud and/or act out the first Torah text, "Joseph the Dreamer" (Genesis 37:1-10) on page 67. Then have the students read and complete "Joseph's Two Dreams" on page 68 and "Sibling Rivalry" on page 69. Stimulate discussion by asking the students whether they relate more to Joseph or to Joseph's brothers. Ask them to specify the aspects with which they associate themselves. Have the students make suggestions that might help alleviate future misunderstandings between siblings. Ask: "What mistake did Jacob make in raising his children? Why should he have known better? Does favoritism by parents occur in real life?"

DREAM 1

The eleven bundles of wheat are symbols for <u>Joseph and his brothers</u> .

The dream predicts that <u>all the brothers will obey and worship Joseph</u> .

DREAM 2

The eleven stars are symbols for _Joseph's brothers_ .

The sun is a symbol for _Joseph's father_ .

The moon is a symbol for _Joseph's mother_ .

The dream predicts that _they will all bow down to Joseph_ .

Closure

3. Have the students read and complete "What about Dinah?" on page 70. You may wish to use the following questions to stimulate discussion:

   • Why do we read so little about Dinah in this story?

   • What would Dinah say about the hostility between her brothers?

4. Have the students read the Torah text on page 71 and complete the activity on page 72. Ask the students: "To what extent did Joseph bring this situation upon himself? What were Reuben's and Judah's motives in trying to act on Joseph's behalf? Why did Jacob tear his clothes when he heard that Joseph had been killed? How might the act of *keriah*—'tearing' a garment—benefit a person who has just heard bad news? What other Torah stories have you read that tell about how people responded to death and dying?"

JOSEPH BELIEVED DEAD

In a tragic turn of events, Joseph, the son of Jacob, _is assumed to be dead_ .

Evidence found at the scene of the tragedy included _his bloody robe_ .

Our reporters were able to reach Jacob, the father of Joseph. Although the old man was clearly upset, he told us it appeared that _a wild animal had eaten his son_ .

During a recent interview Joseph's eldest brother Reuben said that _all the brothers hated Joseph and had plotted to kill him_ .

When confronted by our reporters, another brother, Judah, admitted that _Joseph was actually thrown into a pit and then sold_ .

In related news, _a caravan of Ishmaelite_ traders have been seen in the region.

◼ *50* ◼

Enrichment Activities

1. Have the students reenact the story told in Genesis 37. Encourage them to introduce the character of Dinah into the story, using some ideas from the activity on page 70.

2. Play a recording of Tim Rice and Andrew Lloyd Webber's *Joseph and the Amazing Technicolor Dreamcoat* (Polydor, 1993) for the class. You may wish to play only the beginning of the story for this lesson, saving the second half for the next chapter.

3. Have the students discuss the role of jealousy in the stories of Joseph and his brothers, Jacob and Esau, and Cain and Abel, as well as how jealousy can cause conflict between family members and between friends. Encourage the students to explore the causes of and possible solutions for jealousy.

Joseph in Egypt

Chapter Summary

The dramatic story of Joseph's reunion with his brothers and his father concludes the readings from the Book of Genesis. The Torah texts highlight how Joseph was able to rise above adversity by staying true to his principles.

Objectives

- List changes that take place in nature and people.

- Identify passages from the Torah text that illustrate the importance of caring for others.

Major Themes

- Joseph exercises his skill as a dream interpreter.

- Joseph demonstrates the ability to respond positively to adversity. While he's Potiphar's servant, Joseph holds fast to his principles and is thrown into prison. But by persisting in doing what is right, Joseph rises to the position of prince.

Key Terms

Pharaoh פַּרְעֹה	A ruler of ancient Egypt. Although *Par'oh* is a Hebrew term, it may be derived from the ancient Egyptian *pr-'o*, meaning "great house." It may also be related to the Hebrew verb *para,* meaning to "let alone" or to "uncover."
Famine רָעָב	From the Hebrew root *ra'ev,* which means "hungry." A famine is a severe food shortage that affects a nation or city.

Background for the Teacher

1. Because this chapter contains several Torah texts, you may either wish to limit discussion during the lesson or assign part of the chapter as enrichment reading before class in order to insure that all the material is covered.

2. You may find explaining the behavior of Potiphar's wife embarrassing. Without going into graphic detail, try to convey the difficult situation in which Joseph was placed. Young people will likely sense that in asking Joseph to love her, Potiphar's wife was violating her relationship with her husband. You will have to explore this narrative carefully, taking into account the class dynamic and the level of the students' maturity.

Methodology

Introduction

1. Begin by saying that this is the final lesson in the Book of Genesis. It tells the rest of the story about Joseph. Point out that when the students first met Joseph at the beginning of Chapter 10, he was a spoiled and arrogant young man. At the beginning of this chapter, he is a slave in Egypt. Now—just when it seems as if life is at its lowest point for him—Joseph finds that things can get even worse. But no matter how bad his situation becomes, Joseph holds fast to his principles and eventually becomes the most powerful man in Egypt.

Learning Activities

2. Have the students read "A Slave in Egypt" on page 74. Invite students' questions. Ask: "Why did Joseph refuse Potiphar's wife? What does Joseph's reaction say about his character? Has anyone ever told a lie about you that got you into trouble? How did you feel at the time?"

3. Have the students read and complete "Joseph the Dream Interpreter" on pages 75 and 76. Then tell the students to read "Pharaoh's Dreams" on page 77.

4. Discuss with the class why it is necessary to plan for the future. Today we are concerned with the availability of clean water, clean air, open spaces, natural habitats for wildlife, forest preservation, etc. Have the students generate a list of some of the ways in which we—as individuals,

families, communities—can help plan and prepare for the future (e.g., by recycling, reusing items, using resources sparingly, composting, etc.).

5. Have the students read "A Famine in Canaan" on pages 78 and 79. You may wish to use the following questions to generate discussion:

   • What unusual things did Joseph do in this Torah text?

   • Why did Joseph keep his identity secret from his brothers?

   • Did Joseph want to test his brothers?

   • Did Joseph test his brothers to make them do something he knew would be hard?

   • Why was Jacob so protective of Benjamin?

   • Do parents sometimes forbid their younger children from doing things that they allow their older ones to do?

6. Have the students read "The Second Visit" on pages 80 to 82 and complete the activities on pages 83 and 84. Generate discussion by asking why Joseph "framed" his brother Benjamin by having the cup put inside his bag.

Closure

7. According to tradition, whenever a group completes reading a book of the Torah, they exclaim: *Chazak, chazak, venitchazek* חֲזַק חֲזַק וְנִתְחַזֵּק, which means "Be strong, be strong, and let us strengthen one another." Locate the end of Genesis in a *Sefer Torah* or in Plaut's *The Torah: A Modern Commentary*. Have a student or students read the final verse(s). Then have the class proclaim in unison, *Chazak, chazak, venitchazek.*

   You may also choose to include an additional ritual borrowed from Simchat Torah. Take out a *Sefer Torah* and lead the students in a *hakafah*—a march around the room or the building— holding the scroll.

8. Have the students complete the "Genesis Crossword Puzzle" on page 85.

Genesis Crossword Puzzle

Now that you've completed your study of the Book of Genesis, review all that you've learned by solving this puzzle.

Across

1. Jacob's father-in-law.
4. Story of the binding of Isaac.
5. Abraham's original name.
7. Meaning of *tzedakah*.
9. Rachel to Joseph.
10. Abraham's nephew.
11. Abraham's father.
12. Before you can be forgiven, you must say, "I'm _____."
15. Torah is a Tree of _____.
18. A story that interprets and explains.
19. Forgiveness.
20. Agreement.

Down

1. What Sarah did when she heard that she was going to have a baby.
2. Ceremony of circumcision.
3. Abraham's grandfather.
4. What Noah took into the ark.
6. A *mitzvah* is a Jewish _____.
7. Seventh day: a day of _____.
8. To cut lamb's wool.
11. Righteousness.
13. Eve ate from the Tree _____ Knowledge.
14. Isaac's wife.
16. He walked with God and built an ark.
17. Joseph, after his brothers abandoned him, became a _____.
19. Isaac's mother.

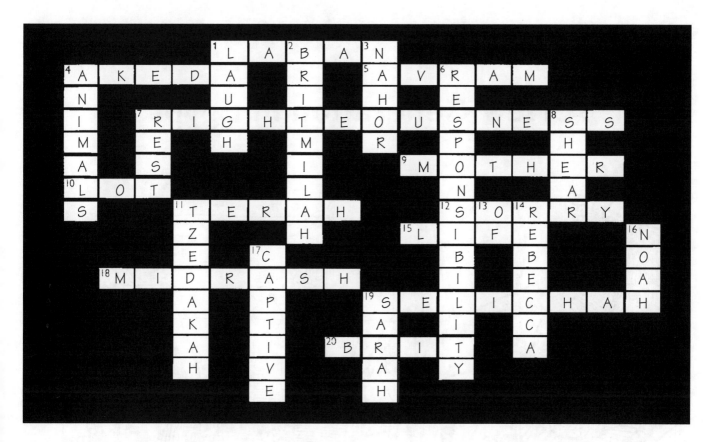

Enrichment Activities

1. Read and discuss the story "Honi and the Carob Tree" in *Sidrah Stories* by Steven M. Rosman (New York: UAHC Press, 1989).

2. Examine current events that pertain to famine, world hunger, and food allocation. Visit a local food bank or soup kitchen.

A New Generation in Egypt

Chapter Summary

In this chapter the students begin reading from the second book of the Torah, Exodus. This chapter includes Torah texts from the first two chapters of Exodus. They establish the link between Joseph's generation and that of Moses.

The period of Israelite slavery in Egypt is similar to the life of Joseph in that both depict the transition from slavery to freedom. During this dark period in our history, Moses provided our ancestors with a spark of hope.

Objectives

- Identify female heroes in Jewish history, including Shiphrah, Puah, and Miriam, and recall their heroic deeds.

- Recognize that Jewish tradition teaches that the survival of the Jewish people has often required acts of courage.

Major Themes

- Like the Israelites during their early years in Egypt, Jews in non-Jewish lands have often prospered and lived harmoniously with the non-Jewish community.

- At times Jews have experienced instances of persecution and anti-Semitism. When a new king arose over Egypt, persecution of the Israelites began.

- Heroes emerge from the midst of dire situations, such as anti-Semitic outbreaks.

Key Terms

Midwife מְיַלֶּדֶת	A woman who assists in birthing. The Hebrew term *meyaledet* comes from the same root as *yeled*, "child," and means "one who brings forth children."
Hero גִּבּוֹר	A hero is a person who behaves exceptionally—above and beyond the norm—by acting bravely and at personal risk in defending people and/or principles.
Anti-Semitism	A hostility toward or hatred of Jews that ranges from discrimination to organized violence and even genocide.

Background for the Teacher

1. The topic of anti-Semitism and prejudice cannot be addressed adequately in one lesson. While an in-depth study of anti-Semitism and the Holocaust is recommended for higher grades, at this level it is appropriate to present and consider the following: (a) anti-Semitism exists even today; (b) anti-Jewish discrimination has existed through different periods of history; (c) particularly in times of discrimination, individuals are challenged to act heroically.

2. Adverse conditions often produce heroes. Without a cruel Pharaoh there would not have been a Moses. Had Antiochus not persecuted the Jews, there would have been no Maccabees.

Methodology

Introduction

1. Begin with a discussion of the miracle of Jewish survival. If this lesson falls on or near Chanukah, relate the story of the Maccabees to that of the Israelites' survival in Egypt. You may wish to open and stimulate the discussion in the following way:

> The Jewish people have existed for almost four thousand years. That is twenty times longer than the existence of the United States and Canada, and forty times longer than that of the former Soviet Union. Every so often, other nations have challenged the Jews' very existence. The Amalekites, the Philistines, Egypt, Babylon, the Syrian Greeks, the Romans, and Hitler's Germany have all tried to destroy the Jews. But the Jews have survived and all of their would-be destroyers are gone. How have the Jews survived the many attempts to annihilate them?

Mark Twain wrote:

> The Egyptian, the Babylonian, and the Persian rose filled the planet with sound and splendor, then faded to dream stuff and passed away. The Greek and the Roman followed and made a vast noise, and they are gone. Other peoples have sprung up and held their torch high for a time, but it burned out, and they sit in twilight now or have vanished. The Jew saw them all, beat them all, and is now what he always was, exhibiting no decadence, no infirmities of age, no dulling of his alert and aggressive mind. All things are mortal but the Jew; all other forces pass, but he remains. What is the secret of his immortality?

That the Jews have survived for so long is a miracle, like the miracle of Chanukah. Part of the miracle is that each time they were challenged, heroes like the Maccabees rose up and defended the Jewish values. In this lesson you will read about another such time that occurred in the land of Egypt several years after the days of Joseph and his brothers.

Learning Activities

2. Have the students read "The Israelite Nation in Egypt" on page 87 and complete "The New Pharaoh" on page 88. You may wish to use the following questions to stimulate discussion:

   • What is meant by the statement "A new king arose… who didn't know Joseph"?

   • What is anti-Semitism?

   • What are some examples of anti-Semitism?

   • What are some reasons for anti-Semitism?

The New Pharaoh

During the time of Joseph, Pharaoh and his people liked and appreciated the Israelites. What caused them to change? Why did they begin to fear the Israelites?

<u>Because there were so many Israelites in Egypt, Pharaoh was afraid</u>
<u>that in time of war, they would side with Egypt's enemies.</u>

Pharaoh tried three different ways to control the growth of the Israelites. Go back and find the ways. Then list them below.

1. <u>He set masters over them and forced them into slavery.</u>
2. <u>He ordered the Hebrew midwives to kill the Hebrew boy babies.</u>
3. <u>He ordered that every Hebrew boy baby be thrown into the Nile.</u>

3. Have the students read and complete "Shiphrah and Puah: Heroic Midwives" on page 89. You may wish to use the following questions to generate discussion:

- The text says that the midwives ignored Pharaoh's ruling because they feared God. Why would their fear of God cause them to ignore Pharaoh's orders?

- The textbook calls Shiphrah and Puah "heroic midwives." What does the word *heroic* mean? What makes these women heroic?

4. Have the students read "Moses: A Hero Is Born" on page 90 and "Meet Miriam" on page 91 and then complete the activity for the latter.

Closure

5. Write the following advertisement on the chalkboard:

> *Wanted: Hero*
> *to save a people from slavery*
> *and lead them in becoming a free nation.*
> *Job description available upon request.*

Tell the students that a job description enumerates the personal traits and specific duties that an applicant should have. For example, the job description of a student might include the following: someone who pays attention in class, completes homework on time, asks questions when appropriate, gets along well with others, etc.

Divide the class into groups of two or three. Have each group write a job description of a hero that fills the specific needs stated in the above ad and includes at least five character traits and/or duties. Post finished job descriptions around the classroom.

Enrichment Activities

1. The story of Moses' early years as an Egyptian noble parallels the stories of other literary heroic figures with secret identities. Oedipus, Sleeping Beauty, Snow White, Clark Kent (Superman), and Luke Skywalker (*Star Wars*)—each was raised far from his or her biological home. Have the students explore some of these heroes and compare their background, personality, and heroic deeds with those of Moses.

2. Have the students write diary entries by pretending to be Miriam, the midwives, or Pharaoh's daughter.

Moses Learns about Responsibility

Chapter Summary

This chapter tells the story of how Moses—now a young man—confronts the issue of justice in Egypt and Midian. The students will explore the value of responsibility and look for parallels between their own struggles and the moral conflicts of Moses.

Objectives

- Analyze selections from Jewish literature, including the *Tanach*, that tell how to resolve situations involving individual and group conflict.

- Define *making an ethical decision* as "choosing the right thing to do."

Major Themes

- In this chapter Moses calls himself "a stranger in a strange land" and shows us how the Jew throughout the ages has been able to live harmoniously as a stranger (i.e., someone different, a member of a minority) in predominantly non-Jewish countries like Midian.

- Moses' struggles typify our own struggles with ethical decisions. He shows us that choosing between right and wrong is not always easy.

Key Term

Stranger

גֵּר

The term *ger* meant "foreigner" or "alien" in the time of Abraham and Moses. In later years it has also come to mean a "non-Jew who has decided to join the Jewish people" or a "convert."

Background for the Teacher

1. About Jethro. Exodus 2:16 tells us that Moses' future father-in-law was a priest of Midian. Exodus 2:18 calls him Reuel, and Numbers 10:29 refers to him as Hobab son of Reuel. The Midianites were distant cousins of the Israelites. Little is known about what kind of priest Jethro was. Some interpreters, referring to Numbers 12:1 in which Zipporah is called a Cushite woman, have suggested that Zipporah, Jethro's daughter and Moses' wife, was Ethiopian and possibly black.

Methodology

Introduction

Begin with a discussion of ethical dilemmas and ethical decisions. Have the students consider the following scenario:

> During recess you decide to go back into the classroom to get your jacket. When you enter the room, you see an older student taking money from someone's desk. The thief warns you not to tell anyone what you saw. If you do, he or she will come after you.

Then ask the students the following questions:

- What are your choices? What are the possible responses to the situation? (tell on the thief or keep quiet)

- What would be the end result of each choice?

- Which choice is the "right" one?

Now present the following scenarios and after each one ask the three questions above.

> The friend who sits beside you in class has been absent because of a family trip. Now he or she is behind in math. When the teacher steps out of the room during a weekly math quiz, your friend whispers, "Let me copy your answers."

> You are walking home from school alone. As you pass an alley, you hear screaming and see two older kids beating up one of your classmates.

After brief discussions of the three scenarios, ask the students whether it was easy or difficult to make the decision about what to do in each case and to explain their answer. Ask them whether they have ever had to make similar decisions.

Explain to the students that decisions about right and wrong are called ethical decisions. Such decisions almost always involve making a choice that could help or hurt someone. The right decision is not always easy and clear. Sometimes we have to wrestle with the choices, just as

Jacob wrestled with the angel in Chapter 9. Chapter 13 is about some of the ethical decisions with which Moses struggled.

Learning Activities

2. Have the students read "A Stranger in a Strange Land" on page 93 and identify and discuss the two ethical dilemmas faced by Moses in the Torah text. (what to do about the Egyptian who was beating the Hebrew and what to do about the two Hebrews who were fighting) Ask the students: "What were Moses' choices in each case? What were the possible consequences of each of these choices? Why did Moses do what he did?"

3. Have the students read and complete "From Egypt to Midian" on page 94 and "Choosing between Right and Wrong" on pages 94 to 96. Below is the completed chart for the activity that appears on page 96 of the text.

	What did Moses see?	What was the ethical question that Moses had to answer?	What did Moses decide to do?	Do you think that Moses did the right thing?	How did this decision change Moses' life?
On the first day that Moses went out to see his people…	He saw an Egyptian beating a Hebrew slave.	He had to decide whether he should try to stop the Egyptian.	He killed the Egyptian and hid his body.		
On the second day that Moses went out to see his people…	He saw two Hebrews fighting.	He had to decide whether he should stop them.	He tried to stop them from hitting each other.		
On the day that Moses went to the well in Midian…	He saw that shepherds did not allow the women to use the well.	He had to decide whether he should help the women use the well.	He chased away the shepherds.		

Closure

4. Sometimes people act wisely on their own without soliciting advice and suggestions from others. Other times people make mistakes in not consulting others.

   Moses tended to make his own decisions without consulting other people. Ask the students: "Do you think that making ethical decisions is easier if you have to make them by yourself or if you can ask the advice of other people?"

Enrichment Activities

1. The Torah tells us little about Moses' childhood. *Midrashim* about Moses' early life can be found in Lillian Freehoff's *Bible Legends: An Introduction to Midrash*, Volume 2: Exodus (New York: UAHC Press, 1988, pages 1 to 10) and Steven M. Rosman's *Sidrah Stories*, pages 44 to 47. Have the students read and/or listen to these selections and then create their own *midrashim* about Moses' youth. *Bible Legends* also contains a *midrash* about Moses' early days in Midian (Volume 2: Exodus, pages 11 to 20).

2. Invite a rabbi or guest speaker to talk to the class about the evolution of the word *ger* and about the role of Jews-by-choice in the Jewish community.

The Burning Bush

Chapter Summary

The narrative of Moses and the burning bush shows us how one person experiences the divine. Moses' experience dramatizes how difficult it is to respond to God's call. The subjects of spiritual encounter, responsibility, and God's names are explored.

Objectives

- Identify selections from Jewish literature, including the *Tanach*, that illustrate the importance of caring for others.

- Associate the word *miracle* with critical moments in Jewish history.

Major Themes

- The Torah tells us that through the miracle of a burning bush, God called on Moses to liberate the Israelites from Egypt.

- Moses teaches us how to worship God through gentle acts of kindness to animals and by appreciating nature.

Key Terms

Tza'ar Ba'alei Chayim

צַעַר בַּעֲלֵי חַיִּים

"Concern for living beings," or "kindness to animals." The Bible and Talmud provide numerous rules and guidelines to protect animals from suffering.

Ehyeh-Asher-Ehyeh

אֶהְיֶה אֲשֶׁר אֶהְיֶה

"I Will Be Who I Will Be." God responded with this name when Moses asked, "Who shall I say sent me?"

Background for the Teacher

1. In this story God has several names:

   יְהֹוָה, YHVH, "God Is," or "Infinite God"—God's personal name, not spoken but read as *Adonai* אֲדוֹנָי; often abbreviated יְיָ—and *Ehyeh-Asher-Ehyeh*, "I Will Be Who I Will Be." The name *Ehyeh-Asher-Ehyeh* is open to a variety of translations and interpretations (see Plaut, *The Torah: A Modern Commentary*, pages 404 to 406).

2. Regarding *Kohanim* and *Levi'im*. The tribe of Levi, to which Moses and Aaron belonged, became the priestly tribe of the Israelites. Most priestly roles were performed by a small group of Levites, the *kohanim*, which consisted of Aaron and his descendants. See Chapter 17 for more information about the role of the priests.

Methodology

Introduction

1. Ask the students to hold up their hand if their answer is Yes to the following questions regarding the appreciation of nature:

   - On your way to religious school this morning, how many of you rode past some trees?

   - How many of you actually saw trees today and are not just remembering them from other times and places?

   - How many of you not only saw trees but really looked at them? Did you look at a particular tree today?

   - Do you know what type of tree you were looking at? Do you know how many branches it had or how long it might have been there?

   By this time the number of raised hands will have dwindled. Continue the lesson by pointing out the following to the students: "All of us see beautiful things every day. But most of the time

◨ 65 ◨

we take them for granted. We are too busy. We are thinking about other things, or we are just not paying attention. In this chapter you will learn that it is a *mitzvah* to pay attention."

2. Introduce the chapter in the following way:

Imagine that God were trying to tell you something, but you were not paying attention. Chapter 14 is called "The Burning Bush." In it God speaks to Moses through a miracle. The miracle is not that a bush is on fire but that the bush is not being consumed by the flames.

If you've ever watched a log burning in a fireplace or camp fire, you know how long it takes for the log to burn up. How much attention must Moses have paid to the bush to realize that it was not burning up?

Learning Activities

3. Have the students read "God Calls on Moses" on pages 98 to 100. Follow the reading with a brief discussion that reviews the main points of the story. You may wish to use the following questions:

- By what means did God speak to Moses in this story?

- How much attention must Moses have paid to have noticed that the burning bush was not burning up?

- Why a burning bush? Why not something more dramatic, like a volcano or at least a large tree?

- If the bush is a symbol, what might it represent?

- Why was Moses told to remove his sandals?

- What was God's reason for contacting Moses? What did God want Moses to do?

- Did Moses want to do what God was asking of him?

- How many times did Moses try to talk his way out of the job that God asked him to do?

- Why do you think God chose Moses?

4. Have the students read and complete "Moses the Shepherd" and "Watching for God's Wonders" on pages 101 and 102. Ask the students to share their responses to the two activities.

5. Have the students read and then complete "The Reluctant Prophet" on pages 102 and 103. Review students' responses to the activity and then ask the students why Moses was uneasy about being God's spokesperson. Ask: "What previous experiences did Moses have that might have made him wary? Are some people naturally inclined to avoid responsibility?"

MOSES' ARGUMENTS	GOD'S RESPONSES
Who am I? Why should I go to Pharaoh? Why did you choose me to free the Israelites from Egypt?	I will be with you. And when you have freed the people from Egypt, you shall worship God at this mountain.
When I go to the Israelites and tell them, "The God of your fathers has sent me to you," they will ask me, "What is God's name?" What will I tell them?	Ehyeh-Asher-Ehyeh, I Will Be Who I Will Be. This you shall say to the Israelites, "Ehyeh has sent me to you."
But what if they do not believe me and won't listen to me? They will say, "God did not appear to you."	God asked, "What is in your hand?" Then God told Moses to throw his rod on the ground, and it became a snake.
O God, I am not a good speaker. I am slow of speech and slow of tongue.	Who gives a person speech? Who makes a person dumb or deaf, seeing or blind? Is it not I, God? I will be with you when you speak. I will tell you what to say.
Can't you send someone else?	Adonai became angry with Moses and said, "I know that Aaron speaks well. You and he will meet, and you shall speak to him. You will tell him what to say. He shall speak for you to the people."

Closure

6. Have the students depict the story of the burning bush artistically. Provide them with construction paper, crayons, pencils, pens, and/or paint. Pictures should illustrate the main points of the story, including the different desires and motivations of God and Moses.

Enrichment Activities

1. Lawrence Kushner's *The Book of Miracles: A Young Person's Guide to Jewish Spirituality* (New York: UAHC Press, 1987) contains a unit about seeing. Chapters 1 and 2 are brief and address many of the same topics as this lesson does. Read them as an alternative or as a supplemental introduction or conclusion to this lesson.

2. The Bible contains many instances of ways in which people have perceived God's presence in nature. Note in particular Psalms 8, 89, 104, and 148. Read one or more of these poems and ask the students to compare the ways in which the poet is "paying attention" to God.

3. Have the students take turns playing the role of Moses and God in the Torah text "God Calls on Moses." Instruct each student who plays Moses to improvise his or her own response to God's call. Discuss the various responses. Tell the students to imagine themselves in Moses' situation. Ask: "How would you respond to being called by God to be a prophet?"

4. Prophets in the *Tanach* sometimes try to refuse God's mission for them. Divide the class into groups and assign each group a reluctant prophet to report on. Possible prophets include Jeremiah (Jeremiah 1:4-10), Jonah (Jonah 1:1-3), and Isaiah (Isaiah 6:1-13).

◨ ◨ ◨ ◨ ◨ ◨ ◨ **CHAPTER FIFTEEN** ◨ ◨ ◨ ◨ ◨ ◨ ◨

The Exodus

Chapter Summary

The story of the Israelites' Exodus from slavery is a paradigm for both political and personal liberation. It is the story of the Israelites' transition from a tribe to a nation, and its narrative is the basis for the *haggadah* read at the Pesach seder. Chapter 15 describes such wonders as the ten plagues and the parting of the Red Sea. But the real miracle of the story is the attainment of the Israelites' freedom.

◨ *69* ◨

Objectives

- Recall selections from Jewish literature, including the *Tanach*, that tell about the festivals.

- Identify events in ancient and modern Jewish history that illustrate assertive behavior on the part of Jews.

- Associate the word *miracle* with critical moments in Jewish history.

- Associate the concepts of freedom and slavery with the festival of Pesach.

Major Themes

- In recalling the story of the Exodus from Egypt, we affirm Jewish peoplehood and the Jewish value of freedom.

- The story of the Exodus and the celebration of Pesach are intertwined.

Key Terms

Exodus
יְצִיאָת מִצְרָיִם

"Departure from Egypt." The story of the Israelites' liberation from slavery in Egypt.

Succoth
סֻכּוֹת

From the word *sukah* סֻכָּה, meaning "protection" or "covering." This term is usually used to describe the structures built for the festival of the same name. In this case, a town is named Succoth in remembrance of God's protection.

Sea of Reeds
יַם-סוּף

The name given in the Torah for the place at which the Israelites crossed over (see Background for the Teacher, item 2, below).

Background for the Teacher

1. Origin of Pesach. The Torah text "The Ten Plagues" on pages 108 and 109 introduces and explains many of the traditions associated with Pesach. Scholars have suggested that these traditions actually predate the story of the Exodus and that the Feast of Matzot and the Feast of Pesach—both agrarian festivals—were originally two separate celebrations that have been joined and transformed via the Exodus story.

2. The Sea of Reeds. Many translations call this body of water the Red Sea, based on a conjecture about the point at which the Israelites crossed into freedom. The map in Plaut's *The Torah: A Modern Commentary,* page 378, suggests several more probable theses about the location of the Sea of Reeds.

3. The story of Miriam and the women dancing at the Sea of Reeds (Exodus 15:20-21) is brief and usually not discussed in most schools. According to a *midrash* (*Exodus Rabbah*), God took the Israelites out of Egypt because of the pious women of that generation.

Methodology

Introduction

1. Begin with a discussion about the importance of stories and storytelling in Judaism.

Record important points and definitions on the chalkboard. You might wish to use the following or similar questions to generate discussion:

- Why do people tell stories?

- Why do people enjoy listening to stories?

- What can people learn from stories?

- How do people learn from stories?

- Why are some stories better suited for teaching a lesson than others?

Proceed by pointing out this is the last chapter to contain a Torah text that is mostly a story until Chapter 21. As the students learned in Chapter 1, much of the Torah teaches with *mitzvot* instead of stories. Chapters 17 to 21 include some stories but these are used primarily to discuss *mitzvot*.

The story told in Chapter 15 is considered by many people to be the most important one in the Torah. It is the story of how the Jews became a free people.

Learning Activities

2. Have the students read "Let My People Go!" on pages 105 and 106 and complete the activity "Does God Have a Name?" on page 107. Emphasize the fact that as Pharaoh's heart hardened, Moses' job became more difficult. You may wish to use the following questions to review major points:

   - How did Pharaoh respond when Moses and Aaron first asked him to free the Israelites?

   - Since straw made the job of producing bricks easier, why did Pharaoh take away the straw from the Israelites?

   - How did Moses react after Pharaoh took away the straw?

   - How did Pharaoh respond when Aaron threw down his cane and it turned into a snake?

   - What does "Pharaoh's heart hardened" mean?

3. Have the students read "The Ten Plagues" on pages 108 and 109. You may wish to use the following questions to generate discussion:

   - What was the tenth plague?

   - How was the tenth plague similar to a previous decree of Pharaoh's?

   - Which festival does this Torah text describe?

   - What elements of Pesach are found in the story? (roasted lamb, God's passing over the houses of the Israelites, matzah, bitter herbs, search for leaven, remembering the Exodus)

   - Why is it necessary for us to remember the Exodus from Egypt?

4. Have the students read "Crossing the Sea of Reeds" on pages 110 and 111 and "A Midrash" on page 112. Then instruct the students to read and complete "The Exodus and Passover" on pages 112 to 114. Have the students share and discuss their answers to the three questions on page 114.

SHANKBONE	MATZAH

The sacrificial lamb	The bread that had no time to rise during the flight from Egypt

MAROR—BITTER HERBS	CHAROSET

The bitterness of slavery and hard labor	The mortar of the bricks used to build Egyptian palaces and pyramids

SALTWATER	ROASTED OR BOILED EGG

<u>The salty tears of the Israelite</u> <u>slaves</u>	<u>Birth and springtime</u>

5. Have the students read and complete "Miriam's Dance" on page 115. Review with the class some of the ways in which people show their appreciation to God. (by prayer, acts of kindness, donations to synagogues and charitable causes, etc.) Discuss how dance is a form of appreciation and worship.

Closure

6. Celebrate the Exodus from Egypt in song. As a class, learn and sing one or more of the versions of *Mi Chamochah*. *Gates of Song* contains four versions. Review the words and their meaning.

Enrichment Activities

1. There are many *midrashim* about the Israelites crossing the sea, including several explaining the "Song at the Sea," the song that Moses and the Israelites sang after their escape to freedom, which appears on page 111 of the textbook. See Joel Grishaver's *Shema and Company* (Los Angeles: Torah Aura Productions, 1991, pages 144 to 145, 153, and 154) or *Shema Is for Real* (Los Angeles: Torah Aura Productions, 1994, page 27). For additional *midrashim* and related activities, see Lillian Freehof's *Bible Legends: An Introduction to Midrash*, Volume Two: Exodus, Chapters 3 and 4.

2. Because of space constraints, the following two stories were not included in *Torah: The Growing Gift*: The Manna and Quail in the Wilderness (Exodus 16) and The Waters of Meribah (Exodus 17; Numbers 20).

   You may wish to include these texts or a summary of them when you teach this lesson. Note that the story of the Waters of Meribah is repeated in Numbers 20. You may wish to present and/or review that story when you teach Chapter 22.

3. Have the students find the "Song at the Sea" in a *Sefer Torah*. Point out that the text of this song is written differently from the rest of the Torah. Ask the students to suggest possible reasons for the unique layout. Possible answers include: It makes the reader's eyes go back and forth as if he or she were following a wave; the words are parted to show us how the waters parted; it draws our attention to this portion so that we do not forget it.

4. Play and/or learn "Miriam's Song" by Debbie Friedman. (A recording of this song is featured on *And You Shall Be a Blessing*, available from Sounds Write Productions, Inc.) This favorite song of kids emphasizes the important but often overlooked story of the Israelite women.

5. Discuss the use of creative or folk dance as a means of spiritual expression.

The Revelation at Sinai

Chapter Summary

Chapter 16 emphasizes *mitzvot* rather than narrative. God is revealed to the entire people of Israel. The Ten Commandments are given. Most of this chapter, the longest in the textbook, is dedicated to the study of the Ten Commandments.

Objectives

- Identify the Ten Commandments.

- Associate the word *miracle* with critical moments in Jewish history.

- Identify ways in which the Ten Commandments are observed.

Major Themes

- In the forty-year period during which the Israelites wandered in the desert, the people underwent a change and learned many things. Although they began their journey as a purposeless slave nation, they entered Canaan forty years later as a free people united by the Torah.

- In this chapter the students begin a study of some of the *mitzvot* found in the Torah.

Key Terms

Aseret Hadibrot
עֲשֶׂרֶת הַדִּבְּרֹת

The "Ten Sayings" or "Ten Statements." Called the Ten Commandments in English. A set of *mitzvot* that were, according to tradition, inscribed on two stone tablets by God and given to the Jewish people by god's prophet, Moses.

Matan Torah
מַתַּן תּוֹרָה

"Giving of the Torah." The revelation at Sinai.

Background for the Teacher

1. Wanderings in the Desert. In Exodus 13:17-18 we learn that God led the Israelites to freedom in a "round-about" way. Tradition gives us several explanations for why a more direct route was not taken:

   - The text itself tells us that the Israelites did not go by way of the land of the Philistines, with whom violent clashes were likely. But Plaut, in *The Torah: A Modern Commentary*, page 478, points out that this is an anachronism because the Philistines appear to have reached Canaan *after* the Israelites had settled there.

   - A longer route would allow time (forty years) for the slave generation to die, so that the generation entering Canaan would be born free.

   - A longer route would give the Israelites time to receive the Torah and learn the value of its commandments.

2. There is some confusion about how many *mitzvot* we received at Sinai. In Jewish tradition the number is 613. The Ten Commandments presented in this chapter's Torah text are considered the most essential of the 613 *mitzvot* and, according to tradition, are the only ones that were written in God's hand and given directly to the people.

   Noteworthy is the fact that Exodus 34 presents an alternate version of the Ten Commandments, which differs significantly from the first set in Exodus 20.

3. The revelation at Sinai, like the Exodus from Egypt, is an event that is shared by all Jews of every generation. We are told that each generation of Jews should regard themselves as having stood at the foot of Sinai to receive the Torah.

4. You may find it awkward to discuss adultery (the seventh commandment) with young people. However, you will probably discover that most of your students have a fairly clear idea of the meaning of adultery. The original intent of the law forbade a man from sleeping with the wives of other men and forbade a woman from sleeping with anyone other than her husband. Today

we can understand this commandment in broader (and more egalitarian) terms. The commandment prohibits all extramarital sex, emphasizes that marriage and family are holy, and reminds us not to break our promises or bend ("adulterate") our values.

5. The ninth commandment, usually translated "You shall not bear false witness against your neighbor," is different from the third commandment ("You shall not swear..."). This *mitzvah* prohibits gossip or slander, originally understood in the context of courtroom testimony. Today it encompasses a broader scope of concern. It is understood to mean, You shall not do harm to others with careless words.

Methodology

Introduction

1. Begin by asking the students to imagine a world without rules. Point out that while all of us dislike having rules at times, most of us recognize that they are necessary. Ask the students to suggest reasons for rules and how they help us. You may choose to jot down students' responses on the chalkboard. Possible answers include: Rules keep things fair, rules prevent chaos, rules help prevent accidents, rules guide us to become better people.

   Tell the students that in this lesson they will explore a particularly well-known set of rules, the Ten Commandments.

Learning Activities

2. Have the students read "The Revelation" on pages 117 and 118. Review with the students other biblical revelations that they have studied thus far. Possible answers include: Abraham had several revelations, including the three angels who visited his tent and the angel that stopped him from sacrificing Isaac; Jacob had several revelations, including his dream of the ladder and his wrestling experience with the stranger; Moses had several revelations, beginning with the burning bush.

   Tell the students that they will now examine the Ten Commandments, one by one.

3. Have the students read and complete "The First Commandment" and "The Second Commandment" on page 119. Ask the students the following questions:

   • Is the first commandment a *mitzvah*?

   • What does it command of us?

   • How should we interpret the second commandment?

   • What are some examples of modern idols to which we should not bow down?

4. Have the students read and complete "The Third Commandment" and "The Fourth Commandment" on page 120. Invite students' responses to the following questions:

   • What are some of the benefits (to ourselves and/or others) of not "swearing falsely"?

   • What explanation does the Torah give for observing Shabbat?

   • What benefits do we derive from Shabbat for ourselves, our families, and/or others?

5. Have the students read and complete "The Fifth Commandment" and "The Sixth Commandment" on page 121 and "The Seventh Commandment" on page 122. You may wish to use the following questions to stimulate discussion:

   - The Hebrew word for honor is derived from the word *kaveid*, which means "heavy." Is there a connection between the term *heavy* and the value of honoring parents?

   - What does the Torah mean when it says, "…so that you may last for a long time on the land…"? Why is this statement linked to honor?

   - Why is the Torah concerned with murder?

   - Why does the Torah devote a commandment to keeping marriage holy?

6. Have the students read and complete "The Eighth Commandment" on page 122. Then assign "The Ninth Commandment" and "The Tenth Commandment" on page 123. You may wish to use the following questions to stimulate discussion:

   - Why is the Torah concerned with stealing?

   - How is lying about others a type of murder?

   - How is it hurtful both to ourselves and to others to desire what is not ours?

7. Have the students read and complete "Types of Mitzvot" on pages 123 and 124.

MITZVOT	POSITIVE OR NEGATIVE	PERSON/PERSON OR PERSON/GOD	YOUR RANK
I am *Adonai* your God, who brought you out of the land of Egypt.	+	Person/God	
You shall have no other gods beside Me.	−	Person/God	
You shall not swear falsely by the name of *Adonai*.	−	Person/God	
Remember the Sabbath and keep it holy.	+	Person/God and Person/Person	
Honor your father and mother.	+	Person/Person	
You shall not murder.	−	Person/Person	
You shall not commit adultery.	−	Person/Person	
You shall not steal.	−	Person/Person	
You shall not tell falsehoods about other people.	−	Person/Person	
You shall not desire the things that belong to other people.	−	Person/Person	

After the students have filled in the chart on page 124, draw and complete the chart on the chalkboard with the class. Eliminate the Your Rank column on the class chart.

Closure

8. As a creative closure, have the students do any of the Enrichment Activities listed below or complete "My Experience at Sinai" on page 118 of the textbook. Tell the students to include many details about the sights, sounds, smells, and emotions they experienced during their personal experience at Sinai. Ask volunteers to share their story with the class.

Enrichment Activities

1. Divide the students into small groups. Have the members of each group dramatize one of the Ten Commandments, basing their dramatization on one of the stories in the textbook or on another situation.

2. Mitzvah Charades. Put ten pieces of paper (numbered 1 to 10) into a hat or box. Divide the class into small groups of two to four students. Have a person from each group select one piece of paper from the hat. The chosen number denotes the commandment that the person's group must dramatize, using little or no dialogue. The other students must guess which commandment is being portrayed. You may wish to follow each dramatization with a short discussion.

3. Have the entire class create and perform a play in ten acts, with each act representing a commandment.

4. Have the students create a mural depicting the Ten Commandments.

5. Show an excerpt from the film *The Ten Commandments*, directed by Cecil B. DeMille (1956).

6. Have the students listen to and/or learn Debbie Friedman's song "613 Mitzvot." (A recording of this song is featured on *Debbie Friedman Live at the Del*, Sounds Write Productions, Inc.)

7. Point out that the Israelites heard the sound of the shofar during the revelation. Have the students discuss how the sounds of the shofar blasts during Rosh Hashanah help evoke in us the experience of revelation.

A Temple in the Desert

Chapter Summary

The Tent of Meeting is a model both for the Temple in Jerusalem and the synagogue. In this chapter the holy objects of the Temple are discussed. The chapter concludes with the story of the golden calf and the second set of tablets of the Law.

Objectives

- Identify the ritual objects found in the Tent of Meeting, the *mishkan*, and the Holy of Holies.

- Connect aspects of the Tent of Meeting to their counterparts in the Temple in Jerusalem and modern synagogues.

Major Themes

- We can better understand the design of our own synagogue if we study the instructions for the design of the *mishkan* in the Torah.

- The Israelites' worship of the golden calf shows how easy it is to be tempted to worship a god that can be seen and how difficult it is to worship our God who cannot be seen.

Key Terms

Tent of Meeting
אֹהֶל מוֹעֵד

The tent where Moses and sometimes Aaron met with God.

Mishkan
מִשְׁכָּן

"Dwelling." A room within the Tent of Meeting in which the Holy of Holies was located. Often translated as "tabernacle" (from the Latin word for "hut").

Holy of Holies
קֹדֶשׁ הַקֳּדָשִׁים

The inner room of the sanctuary in the Tent of Meeting, where the *Aron Ha'edut* was kept.

Aron Ha'edut
אֲרוֹן הָעֵדֻת

The "Ark of the Pact or Covenant" was a special box or chest in which the tablets of the Law (apparently the Ten Commandments) were stored. The ark was kept in the Holy of Holies and later in the Temple.

Menorah
מְנוֹרָה

A lamp or candelabra. While the term *menorah* can refer to any lamp, in this context it refers to the seven-branched menorah used in the Tent of Meeting.

Ner Tamid
נֵר תָּמִיד

"Eternal Light" or, according to Plaut, "Regular Light." The lamp in the Temple and *mishkan* that faced the Holy of Holies burned regularly.

Cubit
אַמָּה

The length of a forearm, approximately eighteen inches.

Kohen
כֹּהֵן

A Jewish priest. The *kohanim* (plural form) are members of the tribe of Levi and, more specifically, descendants of Moses' brother, Aaron.

Levi
לֵוִי

Members of the tribe of Levi. When the Israelites entered the Promised Land, the *Levi'im* did not receive a portion of land but were instead given certain priestly responsibilities and privileges.

Background for the Teacher

1. The details about the *mishkan*, its floor plan, and its furnishings may be retrojections from the First Temple era of the design of the Temple in Jerusalem onto an earlier period. Historians have noted that the design of the *mishkan*, which mirrors that of the Temple, is far too elaborate a structure to have been built by a people who were still wandering.

2. The Torah is unclear about the distinction between the *mishkan* and the Tent of Meeting. On page 688 of *The Torah: A Modern Commentary*, Plaut suggests that two different traditions probably existed, with one using the first term and the other using the second. The traditional explanation is that the Tent of Meeting was used temporarily until the *mishkan* was built. For

the purposes of the students at this level of study, we teach that the *mishkan*, "tabernacle," was a room in the *Ohel Mo'ed*, the "Tent of Meeting," which housed the Holy of Holies.

Methodology

Introduction

1. Begin with a brief tour of the synagogue. Ask the students to note the objects needed to run a synagogue.

   After you return to the classroom, have the students generate a list of resources that they would need to start a new synagogue. Remind them to include less obvious resources such as electricity, plumbing, a building, custodial care, music, teachers, a rabbi, etc.

   Then have the students prioritize this list of resources from the most important to the least important. You may choose to have students do this exercise individually, as a class, or in groups of two or three.

   Finally ask the students how the synagogue would acquire the objects and resources on their list. Ask: "Can people donate some of the objects? Which ones have to be bought? From where would the money come? How does a synagogue get its funds?"

Learning Activities

2. Have the students read "Holy Places" on page 126. Ask them to compare present-day fund-raising methods with the method used by the ancient Israelites. If possible, show illustrations of the *mishkan*, the First Temple, or the Second Temple.

3. Have the students read and complete "The Ark of the Covenant" on page 127 and "The Menorah" on page 128. Then have the students share their responses.

4. Have the students study the illustration of the Ark of the Covenant on page 127. Then ask them to describe what they see and tell what they find interesting about the ark. Ask: "If you were on the committee appointed to design the Ark of the Covenant, how would you go about selecting a design?" Divide the class into groups of two or three. Tell the students to imagine that their group is an architecture firm. Have the members of each group create a blueprint for the Ark of the Covenant and present their design to the class. Tell them to keep in mind the values of portability, holiness, and beauty.

5. Have the students read and complete "The Altar and Ner Tamid" on pages 128 and 129. After the students have shared their answers to the question about the *Ner Tamid*, ask them to name some objects that symbolize the same values as the *Ner Tamid* does.

The Altar and Ner Tamid

Why is the lamp kept burning at all times? What is the *Ner Tamid* a symbol of?

God commanded that there be an everlasting light at the altar where the priests performed their rituals. It is a symbol that God is ever present and eternal.

6. Have the students read "The Role of Priests" in the box on the bottom of page 129. Discuss the role of the *kohanim* in ancient religious life and compare it to that of present-day rabbis. Have the students generate a list of rabbinical duties and identify those duties that were likely to have been performed by the *kohanim*. Then have the students identify the duties of the *kohanim* that are not performed by rabbis today.

7. Have the students read "The Golden Calf" on pages 130 and 131. You may wish to use the following questions to generate discussion:

   • What did the people ask of Aaron?

   • Why did the people ask for a new god?

   • Why is it surprising that the people made such a request?

8. Have the students read "A Second Set of Tablets" on pages 132 and 133 and then complete "God's Goodness" on pages 133 and 134. Instruct the students to list the characteristics of God delineated in the Torah text ("*Adonai Adonai...* fourth generations"). Then have the students generate a new list that contains additional attributes of God, based on their own understanding of God. Finally discuss the image of "glowing" as a result of an encounter with God.

Closure

9. Ancient Architects. Have each student choose items in the *mishkan* (e.g., the Ark of the Covenant, the menorah, the altar, or the *mishkan* itself) and draw or build a cardboard or clay model of that item. Inform the students that more detailed plans about these items can be found in *The JPS Torah Commentary: Exodus 25-28*, edited by Nahum M. Sarna (Philadelphia: JPS, 1990). Also refer the students to Exodus 37-39.

Enrichment Activities

1. Show slides or photos of the Temple model located in the Holy Land Hotel in Jerusalem.

2. Have a rabbi visit the class to talk about what he or she does. Have the students compare the rabbi's role to that of the *kohen* in the time of the *mishkan* and Temple.

3. Examine and discuss the thirteen attributes of God (see Plaut, pages 663 to 664). Tradition delineates these thirteen characteristics of God from Exodus 34:6-7:

   (1) *Adonai* (i.e., God Was and Is)

   (2) *Adonai* (i.e., God Will Be)

   (3) God (i.e., Being the Most High)

   (4) Full of compassion

   (5) Full of graciousness

   (6) Patient

   (7) Full of kindness

   (8) Truth

   (9) Giving kindness to the thousandth generation

(10) Forgiving failure

(11) Forgiving immorality

(12) Forgiving mistakes

(13) Punishing when necessary

4. Show the students a picture of Michelangelo's sculpture of Moses. Michelangelo, who lived in Italy from 1475 to 1564, misread the verse "his face was beaming." On his statue Michelangelo carved beams or horns coming from Moses' head. The word for "horn" in Hebrew is also the word for "ray of light" (*keren*).

You Shall Be Holy

Chapter Summary

This is the first of three chapters in the Book of Leviticus that are about holiness. Aspects of holiness include the sacrificial offerings made by the Israelites and the rules of *kashrut*. The students will read a Torah text called the Holiness Code (Leviticus 19), compare the Holiness Code with the Ten Commandments, and examine some of the most important *mitzvot* contained in the code.

Objectives

- Identify Leviticus, the third book of the Torah, as a book that is primarily concerned with priestly (Levitical) matters and guidelines for living a holy life.

- Define the terms *offering* and *sacrifice* as the ceremonial bringing of gifts to God.

- List the basic rules of *kashrut*.

- Associate the Golden Rule with the Torah and the concept of *kedushah*.

Major Themes

- During the Israelites' wandering in Sinai and after their settlement in Canaan, they shared gifts of food with God as part of their religious worship.

- We acquire *kedushah* by observing *mitzvot* in our everyday activities. These *mitzvot* provide us with guidelines for which foods are proper, *kosher*, and improper, *treif*.

Key Terms

Leviticus וַיִּקְרָא	A Greek name meaning "Priestly," from the Hebrew *Levi*, the priestly tribe. The Hebrew name for this book, the third of the Five Books of Moses, is Vayikra, "And [God] Called."
Offering קָרְבָּן	A gift joyfully given to God. The Hebrew word *korban* means "that which is brought near [to God]."
Kosher כָּשֵׁר	The term *kosher*, meaning "fit" or "proper," is most often used to describe food that is chosen and prepared according to the rules stated in the Torah and explained in the rabbinic writings.
Terefah טְרֵיפָה	The term for nonkosher food, *treif* in Yiddish. Originally referred to meat that was torn from a living animal.
Holy, Holiness קְדוּשָׁה	The terms *kadosh* and *kedushah* mean "special" or "set apart." They are also translated as "sacred."

Background for the Teacher

1. Problems of Discussing Ritual Sacrifices. Several obstacles make it hard for people today to understand the role of sacrifices in ancient Israel. Among them are the difficulty of grasping the meaning of the word *sacrifice* and comprehending the nature of the offerings.

   In modern jargon *sacrifice* means "giving something up" or "practicing self-deprivation" (e.g., giving up pleasurable activities to help others or giving up certain foods to lose weight). To our ancestors, however, the term *sacrifice* was something altogether different. The word itself comes from a Latin root meaning "make sacred." The Hebrew word *korban* means "that which is brought near [to God]" or "that which is brought to the altar." To aid students' understanding, *Torah: The Growing Gift* uses the word *offering* in place of *sacrifice* whenever the textbook refers to the ancient act of bringing gifts of food to God.

2. The Nature of the Offerings. It is common for modern readers to harbor misconceptions about the ancient practice of offering sacrifices. We tend to assume that this act was primitive, barbaric, cruel to animals, and a waste of food. At best, we regard the practice of offering sacrifices as a kind of bribery of God.

In reality, the act of bringing an offering to God was joyous. The Torah states that God did not need such offerings. On the contrary, they served the needs of the giver. Foods of all kinds were precious to the Israelites. Going to Jerusalem to offer sacrifices was a public event that can be likened to a modern picnic or barbecue. The bringing of meat, grain, or fruit was a happy and sacred event for the entire family. For more on the history of offering sacrifices, see Plaut, *The Torah: A Modern Commentary*, pages 750 to 755.

3. *Kashrut* in Reform Judaism. While early Reform leaders rejected the biblical dietary laws as primitive, this view has been changing over the past several decades. In *Gates of Mitzvah*, pages 40 and 130 to 133, *kashrut* is discussed in the following way:

> Many Reform Jews observe certain traditional dietary disciplines as a part of their attempt to establish a Jewish home and life style. For some, traditional *kashrut* will enhance the sanctity of the home and be observed as a *mitzvah*; for some, a degree of *kashrut* (e.g., the avoidance of pork products and/or shellfish) may be meaningful; and still others may find nothing of value in *kashrut*. However, the fact that *kashrut* was an essential feature of Jewish life for so many centuries should motivate the Jewish family to study it and to consider whether or not it can enhance the sanctity of their home.

4. The guidelines of *kashrut* include:

   - Only certain species of animals—mammals with split hooves that chew their cud, fish with scales and fins, domestic fowl—may be eaten.

   - The mammals and fowl that may be eaten must be slaughtered in a prescribed way to minimize animal suffering and to remove all blood.

   - Blood may not be consumed.

   - Dairy and meat foods must be kept separate.

5. The Holiness Code is the name given by scholars to Chapters 17 to 26 in Leviticus, which contain a collection of *mitzvot* pertaining to personal and civic holiness. Leviticus 19 contains many of the most notable *mitzvot* in the Torah. This portion of Leviticus is designated as the Torah reading for Yom Kippur afternoon.

6. The readings for Chapter 18 culminate in the Golden Rule (Leviticus 19:18). This is the earliest written reference to that rule.

   The Golden Rule has been worded in various ways, including "Do unto others as you would have them do unto you" and "That which is hateful to you, do not do to any person."

Methodology

Introduction

1. Begin by indicating that Chapter 18 introduces a new book of the Torah, Leviticus. On the chalkboard write the English and Hebrew names of the first three Books of Moses:

Genesis	Exodus	Leviticus
Bereshit	Shemot	Vayikra

Ask the students to list the key events in the first two of these books. Fill in the chart with the students' answers or have two teams of students complete the chart.

Genesis Bereshit	Exodus Shemot	Leviticus Vayikra
The Creation Story	Moses	
Noah and the Flood	The Exodus from Egypt	
Stories about the Matriarchs and Patriarchs	The Ten Commandments	
Joseph and His Brothers	The Building of the *Mishkan*	
Etc.	Etc.	

Learning Activities

2. Have the students complete "What Is Holy?" on page 136 and then answer the question for "Gifts to God" on the same page. After the students have read "In Ancient Israel" in the box on top of page 137, ask them to compare modern methods of worship and celebration with the ritual described in "Gifts to God." Comparing making an offering to a picnic or a barbecue held for a religious reason—i.e., to honor God—may help the students to appreciate and understand the rite of ritual sacrifice.

You may wish to use the following questions to stimulate discussion:

- How is bringing an offering like giving *tzedakah*?
- What can a person who brings an offering gain from the act?
- What are some of the similarities and differences between prayers and offerings?

Gifts to God

We act kindly toward others.

We offer prayers.

We give tzedakah (charity) to the poor.

3. After the students have read "Kosher Food" on page 137, have them complete "Is It Kosher?" on page 138. Then have the students read "Milk and Meat," which appears in the box on the

bottom of page 138. Review the major dietary laws stated in the Torah text by asking the students the following questions:

- What kinds of land animals may be eaten?

- What kinds of marine animals may be eaten?

- What kinds of birds may not be eaten?

- What does the Torah tell us about mixing milk and meat?

Supplement the details provided in the text with any or all of the following:

- Families differ in the dietary traditions they observe.

- Reform Judaism respects any level of observance based on knowledge and commitment.

- The purpose of the kosher method of slaughtering birds and land animals is to prevent animal suffering.

- The separation of milk and meat may extend to the separation of dishes and utensils intended for use with dairy and meat foods.

- Fruit, vegetables, grains that have no dairy ingredients, eggs, and fish are considered *pareve*, "neutral"—neither meat nor milk—and may be eaten with either meat or dairy foods.

4. Have the students read "The Holiness Code" on page 139. Tell the students that the Book of Leviticus primarily contains *mitzvot* and that these *mitzvot* pertain to many areas of Jewish life, from worship to personal ethics to holiday celebrations. The theme that unites all the *mitzvot* in Leviticus is holiness.

   Ask the students to list what kinds of *mitzvot* they are likely to find in Leviticus. Add the students' responses to the appropriate column on the chalkboard (see Activity 1, above). Possible answers include: Holiday Observances, Candlelighting on Shabbat, Going to Temple, Special Foods, etc.

5. Have the students complete the first activity for "The Holiness Code and the Ten Commandments" on page 140. The students should include all of the repetitious material. Also inform the students that not all the Ten Commandments are repeated in the Holiness Code. Review together with the students each of the *mitzvot* listed on page 140.

THE TEN COMMANDMENTS	THE HOLINESS CODE
I am *Adonai* your God, who brought you out of the land of Egypt.	I, *Adonai* your God, am holy.
You shall have no other gods besides Me.	N/A
You shall not swear falsely by the name of *Adonai* your God.	You shall not swear falsely by My name.
Remember the Sabbath and keep it holy.	You shall keep My Sabbath.
Honor your father and mother.	You shall respect your mother and father.
You shall not murder.	N/A
You shall not commit adultery.	N/A
You shall not steal.	You shall not steal; you shall not cheat your neighbor; you shall not rob.
You shall not tell falsehoods about other people.	You shall not lie or trick others.
You shall not desire the things that belong to other people.	N/A

6. Have the students complete the second part of the activity on page 141, either independently or in pairs.

Closure

7. Conclude the lesson with a creative assertiveness activity. Tell the students that they are going to create a campaign supporting the value of holiness. Have the students make Be Holy posters using construction paper or oak tag and crayons, ink, or paint. Display the completed posters around the classroom and/or in the school.

Enrichment Activities

1. Discuss with the students what they have learned about the concept of holiness. Write God Is Holy on the chalkboard and ask the students for examples that illustrate this statement. Possible answers include: God is infinite, God created us, God is special, etc.

   Then write Places Are Holy on the chalkboard and have the students provide examples that illustrate this point. Possible answers include: Israel, the synagogue, the *mishkan*, the Holy of Holies, etc.

   Repeat the activity with Times Are Holy (Shabbat, holidays, birthdays, etc.) and Objects Are Holy (*Sefer Torah, Aron Habrit, Ner Tamid, mezuzah,* etc.).

2. By doing *mitzvot,* we bring holiness into our lives. This idea is expressed in the phrase *Baruch Atah* Adonai...*asher kideshanu bemitzvotav*—"Blessed are You, *Adonai*... who makes us holy with *mitzvot.*" Have the students recite the the following blessing:

   בָּרוּךְ אַתָּה יְיָ אֱלֹהֵינוּ מֶלֶךְ הָעוֹלָם
   אֲשֶׁר קִדְּשָׁנוּ בְּמִצְוֹתָיו וְצִוָּנוּ לְהַדְלִיק נֵר שֶׁל שַׁבָּת.

   Baruch Atah, Adonai Elohenu, Melech haolam,
   asher kideshanu bemitzvotav vetzivanu lehadlik ner shel Shabbat.

   Blessed are You, *Adonai* our God, Ruler of the universe,
   who makes us holy with *mitzvot*
   and commands us to kindle the lights of Shabbat.

   Based on the blessing, ask the students to identify how God makes us holy with *mitzvot.*

3. Display a number of packaged food products that bear a label designating kosher supervision (e.g., *hechsher* symbols like (K) and (U)).

4. Have the students look through magazines for pictures of foods. Then instruct the students to clip out the pictures and make a poster or collage that graphically displays foods that are kosher and those that are not.

5. Hold a class barbecue or picnic at which appropriate blessings are said over the food and drinks and the concept of offerings is again discussed.

6. *The Jewish Catalog* by Richard Siegel and Michael and Sharon Strassfeld (Philadelphia: JPS, 1973, pages 4 and 5) opens with a folktale about holiness. Read this story to the students and have them depict it in diagrams or artwork.

The Israelites Celebrate

Chapter Summary

This chapter explores six major biblical holidays—Shabbat, Pesach, Shavuot, Rosh Hashanah, Yom Kippur, and Sukot. As the students study the themes and historical background of each holiday, they are asked to articulate how each one brings special meaning to their own lives.

Objectives

- List the holidays that have their origins in the Torah.

- Identify historical and agricultural themes that apply to each of the biblical holidays.

Major Themes

- Just as places and people can be *kadosh*, so, too, times can be made *kadosh* through the observance of the holy days.

- We can learn more about our people's values by exploring the values associated with the Jewish holy days, for example, freedom, thankfulness, renewal, forgiveness, etc.

Key Terms

Chag
חַג

"Holiday" or "festival." From an ancient word for "pilgrimage."

Pesach
פֶּסַח

"Passover." The holiday that celebrates the Israelites' redemption from Egyptian slavery.

Shavuot
שָׁבוּעוֹת

"Weeks." The Feast of Weeks or Pentecost, the culmination of the period of the seven weeks plus one day of the harvest that starts with Pesach.

Rosh Hashanah
רֹאשׁ הַשָּׁנָה

"Head of the Year." The first of the month of Tishri, known as the Jewish New Year.

Yom Kippur
יוֹם כִּפּוּר

"Day of Atonement." A solemn fast day observed on the tenth day of Tishri.

Sukot
סֻכּוֹת

"Booths." The Feast of Booths or Tabernacles from the Hebrew word for "temporary dwellings."

Background for the Teacher

1. The word *chag* חַג (plural: *chagim* חַגִּים) refers specifically to joyful times. As a general rule, a holiday on which no food is eaten is not called a *chag*. The term *Yom Tov* יוֹם טוֹב or *Yontif* in Yiddish, "Good Day," although less frequently used, applies to both joyful and solemn holidays such as Yom Kippur. The common holiday greeting is *Chag Sameach* חַג שָׂמֵחַ, which means "Happy Holiday."

2. In ancient times families observed the festivals of Pesach, Shavuot, and Sukot by bringing offerings to the Temple in Jerusalem. Thus these three holidays are known as the Three Pilgrimage Festivals—*Shalosh Regalim* שָׁלֹשׁ רְגָלִים or the "Three Foot Days." Each of them has agricultural as well as national and religious meaning, as shown in the chart on the following page.

	AGRICULTURAL MEANING	HISTORICAL MEANING	RELIGIOUS MEANING
PESACH	Spring barley harvest; spring calving offering	The Exodus of the Israelites from Egypt	Freedom, liberation, spring
SHAVUOT	End of barley harvest and beginning of wheat harvest	The revelation at Sinai and the receiving of the Torah	Learning, receiving
SUKOT	Final week of fruit harvest before the first frost of autumn	The protection of the Israelites by God during their wanderings	Protection, Providence, thanksgiving

Methodology

Introduction

1. Ask the students to list times that are special to them. These times may include individual days, periods of several days—such as family vacations or weekends—or shorter periods of time—dinnertime, rest time, even the time of a favorite TV program. Ask the students to identify and share how they feel during these times and to explain what distinguishes these times from others.

Learning Activities

2. Have the students read "Holy Times" on page 143. Then have the class reread this Torah text. After each paragraph have the students identify which holy day is being described. Ask the students if they are familiar with any of the holy days described in the text.

3. Have the students read and complete "Shabbat: A Holy Day Every Week" on page 144. Have them share their thoughts about activities that can make Shabbat a holy time.

4. Have the students read and complete "Pesach" and "Shavuot" on page 145 and "Sukot" on page 147. Review the themes as well as the historical significance of each of these holidays, using the students' input. Have the students list the activities associated with each holiday on oak tag for classroom display, using the following headings: Name of Holiday, Hebrew Date, Themes, Historical Significance. Refer to item 2 of Background for the Teacher and the Torah text on page 143.

5. Have the students read and complete "Rosh Hashanah" and "Yom Kippur" on page 146. Review the themes and observances of each of these holidays. Ask the students to identify some positive aspects of observing the High Holy Days. Possible answers include: lessons that can be learned, positive feelings, the resolution of past errors, and being inspired to do good.

6. Have the students read and complete "Which Holy Day Am I?" on page 148.

Which Holy Day Am I?

Below is a game that tests your knowledge of the holy days. Read the description of each holy day. Then write the name of the correct holy day in the proper space.

I am a holy time for you. I occur on the tenth day of the seventh month. I am a day of total rest. You shall practice self-denial on this day.

Which holy day am I? _Yom Kippur_

I am a festival of freedom. On this holiday God commanded that raised bread should not be eaten. I occur in the spring and remind you that God took you out of Egypt, out of slavery.

Which holy day am I? _Pesach_

I am the only holy day that is mentioned in the Ten Commandments. I remind people of Creation. Although I am only one day long, I occur more often than any other holy day does.

Which holy day am I? _Shabbat_

I am a day for counting days and sheaves of barley. On this holiday God gave the Torah at Sinai. I occur seven weeks and one day after Pesach.

Which holy day am I? _Shavuot_

I am a holiday of loud blasts. I am a serious day, and I remind people of the birthday of the world.

Which holy day am I? _Rosh Hashanah_

On this holiday people "camp out" all week. I am a time during which people say thank you to God for all that they have and eat. On this holiday people shake their branches.

Which holy day am I? _Sukot_

7. Close with a game of holiday charades. Write the names of the six holy days discussed in Chapter 19 on six pieces of paper. Put the pieces of paper into a box or hat. Have a student select one piece of paper and try to communicate the holy day written on it without words. The first student to guess the holy day correctly becomes "it" and selects another piece of paper.

   When all of the pieces of paper have been chosen, repeat the game. You may wish to supplement the six holy days with Rosh Chodesh—the New Moon—Chanukah, Purim, Tu Bishevat, Lag Ba'omer, Tishah Be'av, etc.

Enrichment Activities

1. In the section in the *Mishnah* called "Rosh Hashanah," it is written that there are four new years. Discuss the meaning of the term *new year* with regard to calendars, school years, fiscal years, tax years, etc.

2. Have the students design posters that depict the holy days according to the themes and observances described in the Torah.

3. Have the students compare life-cycle events with those of the year cycle. Help the students to determine which life-cycle events correspond with each of the holy days. Possible answers include: birth with Rosh Hashanah or Pesach; consecration with bar/bat mitzvah; confirmation with Shavuot; a new home with Sukot; retirement with Shabbat.

Counting the People

Chapter Summary

Chapter 20 introduces the Book of Numbers. The students will learn about the census, *tzitzit*—"fringes"—*talit*, and the narrative of Joshua and the scouts who were sent to Canaan.

Objectives

- Identify the Book of Numbers as the fourth book of the Torah, which continues telling the story of the Israelites in the wilderness.

- Identify Joshua and Caleb as two of the scouts who were sent to explore the land of Canaan and as the only two who brought back a hopeful report.

Major Theme

- The narrative of Joshua and the scouts teaches that it is best for people to approach change and a new experience with optimism and faith.

Key Terms

Bemidbar
בְּמִדְבַּר

The Book of Numbers. (Literally, "In the Desert")
The Hebrew name refers to the opening line of Bemidbar, "*Adonai* spoke to Moses in the desert."

Tzitzit
צִיצִת

"Fringes," which are attached to the four corners of a garment. The Israelites are instructed to wear *tzitzit* in Numbers 15:38-40 and Deuteronomy 22:12.

Talit
טַלִּית

A prayer shawl. A four-cornered garment with *tzitzit* on each of its corners. Called *talis* in Yiddish.

Background for the Teacher

1. The Book of Numbers begins with a record of a census taken of the Israelites. Although this book is most often called Bemidbar in Hebrew, in the *Mishnah* and elsewhere it is sometimes referred to as *Chumash Hapikudim,* the "Accounting" volume of the Torah. It is from this minor theme of counting that the book received the name Numbers in Roman times.

2. Plaut divides the contents of Numbers into four sections:

    I. Various laws given at Sinai. (Chapters 1-10)

    II. Stories of rebellion on the way to Canaan. (Chapters 10-20)

    III. The story of Bilam. (Chapters 22-24)

    IV. Instructions and land distribution prior to entry into Canaan. (Chapters 25-36)

Chapter 20 of *Torah: The Growing Gift* is about section II.

Methodology

Introduction

1. You may wish to begin with a discussion of the use of lists. Hold up the class list and ask the students to list the reasons for its usefulness (e.g., to take attendance, to record grades, to know who is in the class, etc.). Ask the students to name other types of lists (e.g., billboard charts of popular music, TV listings, lists of presidents, etc.). Then ask the students to suggest some reasons why people use lists.

    One important reason is to keep records for future reference. Point out that the fourth of the Torah's five books opens with such a list.

Learning Activities

2. Have the students read "Scouts in Canaan" on page 150 and complete "The Land of Canaan" on pages 151 and 152. Then have them discuss their answers. Ask how a person's expectations, both optimistic and pessimistic, can sometimes affect the outcome of a new experience.

3. Have the students read "The Corners of Your Garments" on page 153 and complete "Make Your Own Talit." Display a *talit* (and/or a *talit katan*). Pass it around the class so that the students can see the knots of the *tzitzit*.

Ask the students how a *tzitzit* reminds us of God's *mitzvot*. Have the students share their design for their *mitzvah*-reminder garment.

Closure

4. Have the students create their own prayer shawl, using string and fabric. See *The Jewish Catalog*, pages 51 to 57, or Joel Grishaver's *Tallit, An Instant Lesson* (Los Angeles: Torah Aura Productions, 1985). When the students have completed the project, have them put on their *talit*, saying the appropriate blessing:

בָּרוּךְ אַתָּה יְיָ אֱלֹהֵינוּ מֶלֶךְ הָעוֹלָם
אֲשֶׁר קִדְּשָׁנוּ בְּמִצְוֹתָיו וְצִוָּנוּ לְהִתְעַטֵּף בַּצִּיצִית.

Baruch Atah, Adonai Elohenu, Melech haolam,
asher kideshanu bemitzvotav vetzivanu lehitatef batzitzit.

Blessed are You, *Adonai* our God, Ruler of the universe,
who makes us holy with *mitzvot*
and commands us to wrap ourselves in *tzitzit*.

Enrichment Activities

1. Have the students read the text or a summary of the second chapter of Joshua. Ask: "What are the similarities between this story and the story of Joshua and Caleb's scouting of Canaan?" Have the students compare Joshua and Caleb with the two spies who were sent into Jericho.

2. The logo for Israel's Ministry of Tourism depicts the scouts carrying a giant cluster of grapes. Find and display a copy of this logo or have the students make and present their own design of that scene. Then have the students create travel brochures that encourage the Israelites to continue their journey to the Promised Land.

3. The story of the Waters of Meribah in Exodus 17 is repeated in Numbers 20. This important and interesting story was not included in *Torah: The Growing Gift* because of space constraints. Provide a text or summary of this story as a supplement to this chapter.

CHAPTER TWENTY-ONE

Bilam and His Donkey

Chapter Summary

In this chapter the students read the story of Bilam, a foreign prophet who was hired to curse the Israelites. The story is a parable of hope and fate, of integrity and anti-Semitism. The students will also learn the *Mah Tovu* prayer, which includes a passage from this biblical narrative.

Objectives

- Identify Bilam as a prophet who was hired to curse the Israelites but instead ended up blessing them.

- Associate the *Mah Tovu* prayer with the story of Bilam.

- List reasons why Judaism and the Jewish community are worthy of praise.

Major Themes

- God's message is not restricted to the Jews. The righteous people of all nations can hear God's message and understand God's will.

- The Jews and Judaism possess many beautiful attributes that often elicit both admiration and envy from non-Jews.

Key Term

Mah Tovu
מַה-טֹבוּ

"How lovely." The first words of the first prayer recited in the morning synagogue service.

Background for the Teacher

1. Talmudic rabbis considered the story of Bilam so important that they regarded it as a separate book (see Plaut, page 1170).

2. A talking donkey? Many readers become preoccupied with the miraculous talking donkey. The rabbis considered this phenomenon to be one of the ten miracles preordained by God before the completion of Creation. Several interesting points can be made regarding this event:

   - The rabbis disagree about whether this was an actual or a figurative—symbolic—event.

   - It may have been included in the Torah as comic relief.

   - It is ironic that a supposedly dumb animal could see what a great prophet could not.

   - The irony is not that the donkey spoke but that she saw something that the prophet did not.

3. This story has certain parallels to the Exodus story. Each story is about a non-Jewish leader who fears the growth and strength of the Jewish people. In each story a prophet is summoned—in the first story by God and in the second by Balak. The prophet—Moses in the first story, Bilam in the second—grudgingly agrees to carry out the mission. In each case, the prophet can do and say only what God wills. In both stories the malicious plans of the anti-Semitic ruler are thwarted. The first story marks the beginning of forty years of wandering by the Israelites in the desert. The second story marks the end of that wandering.

Methodology

Introduction

1. Ask the students: "Have you ever been suspicious of another person? Has anyone ever been suspicious of you? What did you feel in both instances? Was the suspicion in each case based on real or imaginary perceptions?"

Learning Activities

2. Have the students read "The Story of Bilam" on pages 155 to 158 and then complete "An Interview with Bilam" on page 158. You may wish to use the following questions to stimulate discussion:

   • How is a prophet like a news correspondent?

   • Why did God at first refuse to let Bilam go to Balak?

   • Why did God allow Bilam to go to Balak after the second visit from the latter's ambassadors?

   • What conditions did God set?

   • What did the donkey see that made her stop on the road?

   • How did Bilam respond when the donkey stopped? Why?

   • What was your reaction when you read that the donkey spoke?

   • What was Bilam's reaction to the angel of God?

   • What had Bilam been hired to say when he saw the Israelite camp?

   • What did Bilam say instead? Why?

   • What might Bilam have realized that made him change his mind?

3. Have the students read the information about *Mah Tovu*, which appears in the box on the bottom of page 159. Locate the *Mah Tovu* prayer in a prayer book (see *Gates of Prayer*, page 51, or *Gates of Prayer for Shabbat and Weekdays*, edited by Chaim Stern, New York: CCAR, 1994, page 47). Discuss why people say this verse right after they enter the synagogue for morning services.

4. Have the students read and complete "Bilam's Curse" on page 160. Ask volunteers to share their answers with the class.

Closure

5. Discuss how you feel when someone who is not a member of your family says something nice about you. Have the students compare that experience with non-Jews saying nice things about Jews. Generate a list of some of the aspects of Judaism that might garner praise from non-Jews.

Enrichment Activities

1. Have the students depict the "curses" of Bilam in a poster or mural.

2. Help the students to learn and sing a musical rendition of *Mah Tovu*.

3. Have groups of students depict the events of the Bilam narrative in story or play form and then read their story version or perform their play for students in the lower grades.

Moses Teaches a New Generation

Chapter Summary

Chapter 22 introduces the final book of the Torah, Deuteronomy. In this chapter the students discover the biblical source of the *Shema* prayer and discuss its meaning for Jews today. The verses that accompany the *Shema* teach us ways in which to remember the message of the Torah.

Objectives

- Identify Deuteronomy as the fifth book of the Torah, which tells about the travels of the Israelites and reviews the *mitzvot* in the Torah.

- Explain the meaning and source of the *Shema* prayer.

Major Themes

- You can use Deuteronomy to review all the events and *mitzvot* that were presented in the previous four books of the Torah.

- Just as Deuteronomy is a repetition of the Torah, the *Shema* and *Ve'ahavta* serve as reminders of the messages of the Torah.

Key Terms

Deuteronomy	Greek for "Second Law." The fifth of the Five Books of Moses, Deuteronomy is called Devarim—Hebrew for "Words"—from the verse "These are the words...."
דְּבָרִים	
Shema	"Listen." The prayer from Deuteronomy 6:4 that serves as the watchword of Judaic monotheism.
שְׁמַע	
Ve'ahavta	The prayer that consists of various Torah texts, starting with Deuteronomy 6:5, and begins, "And you shall love *Adonai* your God...."
וְאָהַבְתָּ	
Mezuzah	Hebrew for "doorpost." A mezuzah is a box or case that contains a small piece of parchment with the words of the *Shema* and *Ve'ahavta* prayers. It is put on the doorposts of a Jewish home.
מְזוּזָה	
Tefilin	Leather prayer boxes called phylacteries, from the Greek. Some Jews observe the commandment to wear these leather prayer boxes on their arm and on their head during the weekday morning prayer service.
תְּפִילִין	

Background for the Teacher

1. The exact meaning of Deuteronomy 6:4, the *Shema,* is not certain. Various translations include:

   • *Adonai* is our God, *Adonai* alone. (Plaut)

   • *Adonai* our God is one *Adonai.* (King James; Revised Standard Version)

   • *Adonai* our God, *Adonai* is One. (*Gates of Prayer*)

2. The *Ve'ahavta* instructs us to love God with all our heart—*lev*—soul—*nefesh*—and being or might—*me'od.* To the ancient Israelites the heart, soul, and being represented our thoughts, feelings, and actions. The heart was believed to be the intellectual center of a person, whereas today it is considered to be the emotional center.

3. Chapter 5 of Deuteronomy repeats the Ten Commandments. This version is virtually identical to that in Exodus 20 (see Chapter 16), with the one major exception being the commandment regarding Shabbat. In Exodus the text says, "Remember the Sabbath," while in Deuteronomy it states, "Observe the Sabbath." The former commemorates the story of Creation. The latter is concerned with our providing rest for our employees because we ourselves were once slaves in Egypt.

Methodology

Introduction

1. Before you begin, tie a piece of string around your forefinger. Then hold up that finger and say, "I've tied this string around my finger. Can anyone tell me why?"

At some point the question should elicit the response "as a reminder" or "to help you remember something." At that point say, "Thank you. That's right. Now I remember. I wanted to talk to you about reminders."

With the students' help, generate a list on the chalkboard of reminders (e.g., calendars, shopping lists, recipes, things-to-do lists, etc.). Discuss how each reminder helps people to remember something. Explain that in this chapter the students will learn about reminders that help us recall important values in the Torah.

Learning Activities

2. Have the students read "Moses Speaks to the Israelities" on page 162 and complete the box on the bottom of the page. Then have them share their method for remembering events and *mitzvot* in the Torah.

3. Have the students read "The Shema" on page 163 and then complete "God Is One" on the bottom of the page. Discuss how the students interpret the *Shema* and whether there is or need be a class consensus on its meaning. Then ask the students: "Is it possible to make a law about love? Can love be legislated? What are some of the ways in which we can show our love for God?"

Discuss the meaning of loving God with all one's heart and with all one's soul and with all one's might (see Background for the Teacher, item 2, above). Generate a Ways to Show Your Love for God list on the chalkboard, based on the points listed in the text.

- Love God with all your heart.
- Love God with all your soul.
- Love God with all your might.
- Take these words (the Torah) to heart.
- Teach them faithfully to your children.
- Speak of them when you stay at home and when you are away.
- Speak of them when you lie down and when you get up.
- Bind them on your hand.
- Put them before your eyes on your forehead.
- Write them on the doorposts of your house.
- Write them on your gates.

Discuss possible reasons and/or interpretations for each of the points on the list.

Closure

4. Have the students complete "Interpreting the Ve'ahavta" on page 165. Then have the students share their creative methods of observing the *mitzvah* "Bind them as a sign on your hand. Let them serve as a symbol on your forehead. Write them on the doorposts of your house and on your gates." As the students present their methods, have them explain how their interpretations remind them of the message of the Torah.

Enrichment Activities

1. Demonstrate putting on *tefilin*.

2. The blessings for putting on *tefilin* can be found in *Gates of Prayer*, pages 48 to 49. Additional details about *tefilin* can be found in *The Jewish Catalog*, pages 58 to 63, and *Teaching Mitzvot* by Rabbi Bruce Kadden and Barbara Binder Kadden (Denver: ARE, 1988, pages 57 to 60).

3. Have the students design their own *mezuzot* to put on the doorpost of their bedroom and their playroom at home. Additional details about *mezuzot* can be found in *The Jewish Catalog*, pages 12 to 14, and *Teaching Mitzvot*, pages 53 to 56.

4. Put a mezuzah on the doorpost of your classroom in a dedication ceremony if a mezuzah is not already affixed there. If there already is a mezuzah on the doorpost, then rededicate the mezuzah with a ceremony. Such a dedication ceremony can be found in *On the Doorposts of Your House*, edited by Chaim Stern (New York: CCAR, 1995, pages 103 to 107).

Moses Says Good-bye

Chapter Summary

We have reached the final chapter of *Torah: The Growing Gift*. In this chapter the students learn about the last days of Moses, the transmission of leadership to Joshua ben Nun, and Moses' death.

Objectives

- Identify Joshua ben Nun as Moses' successor, who was given the task of leading the Israelites into their new land.
- Recognize that Moses' death and burial marked a lonely and humble end for our greatest prophet.
- List ways in which the Jewish people can and do engage in Torah study today.

Major Themes

- Moses provides us with a model of a humble hero even at the time of his death.

- Jewish people are encouraged to study the Torah over and over again throughout their lifetime.

Key Terms

Eulogy הֶסְפֵּד	A speech, usually given at a funeral or memorial service, that describes the good qualities of the person who is being mourned.
Parashah פָּרָשָׁה	The weekly Torah portion, also known by the Aramaic word *sidrah*. The Torah is divided into fifty-four *parshiyot*.
Tanach תַּנַ"ךְ	The Hebrew name for the Bible. An acronym consisting of the first letters of the three parts of the Bible: the Torah, *Nevi'im*—Prophets—and *Ketuvim*—Writings.

Background for the Teacher

1. This chapter includes readings from Deuteronomy 31 and 34. Deuteronomy 32 and 33, which do not appear in the textbook contain two poetic speeches attributed to Moses. The first, called the Song of Moses (Deuteronomy 32), is directed to all the Israelites and recalls their past experiences.

   The second, known as the Blessing of Moses (Deuteronomy 33), contains Moses' final words to the twelve tribes. Each of the tribes is described and blessed in turn.

2. The final chapter of Deuteronomy is perhaps the shortest one in the Torah. But despite its brevity, it conveys a powerfully tender image of a great leader's end.

3. The Hebrew text of Deuteronomy 34:6 does not make it clear who buried Moses. While most interpretations suggest that God buried Moses, the text itself reads, "He buried him...." *Torah: The Growing Gift* translates this line as "He was buried by God," thereby clarifying the text and avoiding the ascription of a gender to God.

4. Theories abound about why Moses was denied the chance to enter Canaan. None of them is altogether satisfying. These theories suggest that the denial of entry to Canaan was Moses' punishment for the following:

   - Moses lost his temper and hit the rock rather than touched it. (Numbers 20)

   - Moses was egotistical (same episode, above) when he said, "Shall *we* get water?..." rather than "Shall *God* get water?..."

   - Moses broke down and gave up hope after the scouts brought back a negative message about Canaan. (Numbers 14)

Methodology

Introduction

1. Begin by asking the students to reflect on the fact that ending an experience is often sad. Ask each student to share some of his or her experiences that came to an end, leaving him or her

sad. Possible answers include: a good movie, a good book, a vacation, a trip, summer camp, the school year, a friendship—when someone was about to move—divorce, death, etc.

Tell the class that this chapter marks the end of not only the Torah but also Moses' life.

Learning Activities

2. Have the students read "Moses Prepares to Die" on page 167. You may wish to use the following questions to stimulate discussion:

   • Why do you think the Torah says that Moses lived to be one hundred and twenty?

   • Why did Moses not cross over into Canaan?

   • Do you think that this was fair?

3. Have the students complete "A New Leader: Joshua ben Nun" on pages 167 and 168. Discuss the meaning of "Be strong and steady."

A New Leader: Joshua ben Nun

Why do you think that Joshua was chosen to be the new leader? What did Joshua do to deserve this honor?

Joshua kept faith in God's promise of a new land for the Israelites.

4. Have the students read "The Final Text" on page 168. Then explain that in ancient Egypt important people were buried in elaborate tombs. Egyptian kings were considered gods. When they died, their bodies were mummified and buried in pyramids. People came and worshiped at these burial places. The Torah does not tell us where Moses was buried. Ask the students the following questions:

   • Do you think that Moses' grave was simple or fancy?

   • Why was his burial so simple?

   • Why is the burial place of Moses unknown?

   • How does the story of Moses' death and burial make you feel?

5. Have the students complete "Moses the Man" on page 169 and "Moses' Last Thoughts" on page 170. Encourage them to reread key passages from the textbook on pages 93, 98 to 100, 105 to 106, 108 to 109, 110 to 111, 117 to 118, 130 to 131, 132 to 133, 150, and 167. Review the ways in which modern Jews continue to read and study the Torah.

Moses the Man

Moses was a protector and a prophet, a leader and a teacher. List some of the things that Moses accomplished in each of these roles.

MOSES THE PROTECTOR

1. He protected a Hebrew slave from being beaten.

2. He protected the daughters of the priest of Midian.

3. He went before Pharaoh and demanded the Israelites' freedom.

4. He protected the Israelites from God's anger after they made the golden calf.

MOSES THE PROPHET

1. He listened to God's call at the burning bush.

2. He received the Ten Commandments at Mount Sinai.

3. He saw God's attributes.

4. God gave Moses the ability to perform miracles.

MOSES THE LEADER

1. He brought the Israelite leaders together to tell them of God's plan.

2. He led the Israelites out of Egypt.

3. He led the Israelites through the Sea of Reeds.

4. He led the Israelites to the Promised Land.

MOSES THE TEACHER

1. He taught the Israelites the Torah.

2. He taught the Israelites about the Jewish holidays.

3. He taught the Israelites the Ten Commandments.

4. He taught the Israelites the laws of holiness.

Closure

6. Have the students read "Reading the Torah" on page 171. Complete the lesson with a *Siyum Hasefer*—"Completing the Book"—ceremony. In unison have the students read the final paragraph of the last Torah text on page 168.

> Never again did there rise in Israel another prophet like Moses. God had singled him out, face to face, for the miracles that God had sent him to do in the land of Egypt and for the awesome power that Moses displayed before all Israel.

Follow the reading by chanting in unison, *Chazak, chazak, venitchazek*—"Be strong, be strong, and let us strengthen one another." Follow this ceremony with refreshments.

Enrichment Activities

1. "May you live to be one hundred and twenty" is a common Jewish wish. There are several interesting ways to derive this number arithmetically. Try multiplying 1 x 2 x 3 x 4 x 5. Try also multiplying 10 (commandments) by 12 (tribes).

2. Have the students read the text of Moses' blessing in Deuteronomy 33, which is not included in the textbook. Divide the students into groups, assign each group a tribe, and have the members of each group depict their tribe in a mural. Then show the students pictures of the Chagall windows and have them compare their renditions with those of that artist.

3. Follow "Reading the Torah" on page 171 with a reading from the beginning of the Book of Joshua, which continues the story of the Israelites from the point at which Deuteronomy ends.

TEACHING SCHEDULE

Chapter 1: The Story of Creation

The Creation of Heaven and Earth (Genesis 1:1-2:3)

    The Order of Creation

    In the Image of God

    The Seventh Day

Class Date(s): _____

Notes

Chapter 2: Adam and Eve

The Garden of Eden (Genesis 2:7-9, 2:15-3:23)

    Stories and Symbols

    Knowing Right from Wrong

Cain and Abel (Genesis 4:1-16)

    The First Murder

Class Date(s): _____

Notes

Chapter 3: Noah and the Flood

The Flood (Genesis 6:5-8:12,20; 9:1-17)

    Noah and His World

    The Rainbow

Class Date(s): _____

Notes

Chapter 4: Abraham's New Direction

Abraham and the Idols

    Being Different

    The Family of Abraham

Go Forth (Genesis 12:1-7)

    Finding New Directions

The Father of Many Nations (Genesis 17:1-19)

    The Covenant

Class Date(s): _____

Notes

Chapter 5: The Testing of Abraham

Revelation (Genesis 18:1-14)

How Do We "See" God?

The Binding of Isaac (Genesis 22:1-14)

The Revelation of the Akeda

Class Date(s): _____

Notes

Chapter 6: From Generation to Generation

The Death of Sarah (Genesis 23:4)

A Wife for Isaac (Genesis 24:1-27)

A Wife for Isaac: A Closer Look

The Generation of Isaac (Genesis 24:63-67; 25:7-11)

Class Date(s): _____

Notes

Chapter 7: Twins

The Birth of Esau and Jacob (Genesis 25:19-26)

All in the Family

Esau Sells His Birthright (Genesis 25:27-34)

The Trick and the Blessing (Genesis 27:1-10, 18-29)

Torah Detective

Write Your Own Blessing

Class Date(s): _____

Notes

Chapter 8: Jacob Leaves Home

The Journey (Genesis 28:10-19)

What Are Dreams?

Jacob's Ladder

Jacob Arrives in Haran (Genesis 29:4-14)

Jacob Marries (Genesis 29:25-30)

Laban's Trick

Class Date(s): _____

Notes

Chapter 9: Jacob Wrestles _____

    Jacob Goes Home

    Making Changes: Teshuvah

    Jacob Becomes Israel (Genesis 32:4-9, 23-32; 33:1-5)

    Who Wrestled with Jacob?

    Selichah: Esau and Jacob Are Reunited

    Class Date(s): _____

Notes

Chapter 10: Jacob's Children _____

    Joseph the Dreamer (Genesis 37:1-10)

    Joseph's Two Dreams

    Sibling Rivalry

    What about Dinah?

    Joseph and His Brothers (Genesis 37:18-34)

    A Torah Times News Report

    Class Date(s): _____

Notes

Chapter 11: Joseph in Egypt _____

    A Slave in Egypt (Genesis 39:1-20)

    Joseph the Dream Interpreter

    Pharaoh's Dreams (Genesis 41:1-30)

    A Famine in Canaan (Genesis 42:1-36; 43:8-9)

    The Second Visit (Genesis 43:16-45:15)

    Joseph Looks Back

    Genesis Crossword Puzzle

    Class Date(s): _____

Notes

Chapter 12: A New Generation in Egypt _____

    The Israelite Nation in Egypt (Exodus 1:1-22)

    The New Pharaoh

    Shiphrah and Puah: Heroic Midwives

    Moses: A Hero Is Born (Exodus 2:1-10)

    Meet Miriam

    Class Date(s): _____

Notes

Notes

Notes

Notes

Notes

Chapter 13: Moses Learns about Responsibility

A Stranger in a Strange Land (Exodus 2:11-22)

  From Egypt to Midian

  Choosing between Right and Wrong

Class Date(s): _____

Chapter 14: The Burning Bush

God Calls on Moses (Exodus 3:1-23, 27-31)

  Moses the Shepherd

  Watching for God's Wonders

  The Reluctant Prophet

Class Date(s): _____

Chapter 15: The Exodus

Let My People Go! (Exodus 5-8:13)

  Does God Have a Name?

The Ten Plagues (Exodus 11-13:3)

Crossing the Sea of Reeds (Exodus 14-15)

  The Exodus and Passover

  Miriam's Dance

Class Date(s): _____

Chapter 16: The Revelation at Sinai

The Revelation (Exodus 19-20:15)

  At Sinai

  The Ten Commandments

  Types of Mitzvot

Class Date(s): _____

Chapter 17: A Temple in the Desert

Holy Places (Exodus 25:1-9)

    The Ark of the Covenant

    The Menorah

    The Altar and Ner Tamid

The Golden Calf (Exodus 32:1-20)

    Aaron and Moses

A Second Set of Tablets (Exodus 33:17-34:7, 29)

    God's Goodness

Class Date(s): _____

Notes

Chapter 18: You Shall Be Holy

    What Is Holy?

    Gifts to God

Kosher Food (Leviticus 11:1-23)

    Is It Kosher?

The Holiness Code (Leviticus 19:1-4, 9-18)

    The Holiness Code and the Ten Commandments

Class Date(s): _____

Notes

Chapter 19: The Israelites Celebrate

Holy Times (Leviticus 23:1-44)

    Shabbat: A Holy Day Every Week

    Pesach

    Shavuot

    Rosh Hashanah

    Yom Kippur

    Sukot

    Which Holy Day Am I?

Class Date(s): _____

Notes

Chapter 20: Counting the People

Scouts in Canaan (Numbers 13:1-14:9)

The Land of Canaan

The Corners of Your Garments (Numbers 15:37-41)

Make Your Own Talit

Class Date(s): _____

Notes

Chapter 21: Bilam and His Donkey

The Story of Bilam (Numbers 22:2-24:13)

An Interview with Bilam

Bilam's Curse

Class Date(s): _____

Notes

Chapter 22: Moses Teaches a New Generation

Moses Speaks to the Israelites

The Shema (Deuteronomy 6:1-9)

God Is One

Interpreting the Ve'ahavta

Class Date(s): _____

Notes

Chapter 23: Moses Says Good-bye

Moses Prepares to Die (Deuteronomy 31:1-23)

A New Leader: Joshua ben Nun

The Final Text (Deuteronomy 34:1-12)

Moses the Man

Moses' Last Thoughts

Class Date(s): _____

Notes

Bock, Jerry, and **Harnick, Sheldon.** *Fiddler on the Roof* (Original Cast Album). RCD1-7060, RCA, 1964.

Borowitz, Eugene. *Understanding Judaism.* New York: UAHC Press, 1981.

Cohen, Barbara. *Molly's Pilgrim.* New York: Lothrop, Lee & Shepard, 1983.

Davidson, Charles. *Gates of Song.* New York: Transcontinental Music Publications, 1987.

Freehoff, Lillian. *Bible Legends: An Introduction to Midrash,* Volume 2: Exodus. New York: UAHC Press, 1988.

Friedman, Debbie. *Debbie Friedman Live at the Del.* Cassette or CD available from Sounds Write Productions, Inc., P.O. Box 608078, San Diego, CA 92160-8078; (619) 697-6120.

_____. *And You Shall Be a Blessing.* Cassette or CD available from Sounds Write Productions, Inc.

Grishaver, Joel. *Shema and Company.* Los Angeles: Torah Aura Productions, 1991.

_____. *Shema Is for Real.* Los Angeles: Torah Aura Productions, 1994.

_____. *Tallit, An Instant Lesson.* Los Angeles: Torah Aura Productions, 1985.

Hamilton, Virginia. *In The Beginning: Creation Stories from Around the World.* New York: Harcourt Brace Jovanovich, 1988.

Jewish Publication Society. *The Holy Scriptures.* Philadelphia: JPS, 1962.

Kadden, Rabbi Bruce, and **Kadden, Barbara Binder.** *Teaching Mitzvot.* Denver: Alternatives in Religious Education, 1988.

Kipling, Rudyard. *Just So Stories.* New York: Doubleday, 1972.

Kushner, Lawrence. *The Book of Miracles: A Young Person's Guide to Jewish Spirituality.* New York: UAHC Press, 1987.

Maslin, Simeon J., ed. *Gates of Mitzvah.* New York: CCAR, 1979.

Plaut, W. Gunther, ed. *The Torah: A Modern Commentary.* New York: UAHC Press, 1981.

Rice, Tim, and **Weber, Andrew Lloyd.** *Joseph and the Amazing Technicolor Dreamcoat* (Cast Album). Polydor, 1993.

Richards, Stephen. *Manginot: 201 Songs for Jewish Schools*. New York: Transcontinental Music Publications, 1992.

Rosman, Steven M. *Sidrah Stories*. New York: UAHC Press, 1989.

Sarna, Nahum M., ed. *The JPS Torah Commentary*. Philadelphia: JPS, 1990.

Siegel, Richard; **Strassfeld, Michael**; and **Strassfeld, Sharon.** *The Jewish Catalog*. Philadelphia: JPS, 1973.

Singer, Ellen. *Our Sacred Texts*. New York: UAHC Press, 1993.

Stern, Chaim, ed. *Gates of Prayer*. New York: CCAR, 1975.

_____. *Gates of Prayer for Shabbat and Weekdays*. New York: CCAR, 1994.

_____. *On the Doorposts of Your House*. New York: CCAR, 1995.